The Secret Life of
Mother Mary

"The many aspects of Mary's spiritual presence have evoked deep communion in cultures around the world. Within this generative tradition, Marguerite now draws from her personal experience with Mary, her 'intuitively infused' scholarship, and her creative spiritual explorations to offer an invitation to a rich engagement with the meanings of Mary."

CHARLENE SPRETNAK, AUTHOR OF *MISSING MARY*

"This book is a radical reinterpretation of the life and training of Mother Mary in the yogic practices of parthogenesis or 'virgin birth.' While much of the focus is on the possibility of a sisterhood of advanced temple initiates trained in the yoga of immaculate conception, this book establishes Mother Mary as a truly enlightened master of wisdom in her own right. Relying heavily on the teachings of the Indian sage Kaleshwar as well as early, little-known gospels, the author delves into sacred mantras, Indian siddhis, 'womb magic,' and spiritual powers. She asserts the belief that Mother Mary was not only Jesus's teacher but also crucial to the success of his miracles and resurrection. In short, she reveals Mary as a master initiate who oversees sacred ceremonies, teaches, heals, casts out demons, and raises the dead, illuminating Mary as a powerful incarnation of the Divine Mother."

TRICIA MCCANNON, AUTHOR OF
RETURN OF THE DIVINE SOPHIA

"A must-read primer for anyone unearthing the women surrounding Jesus Christ and the early Christian movement. Read this book and learn from one of the best. The roles the women played not only shaped but birthed a mystical tradition only now coming to light."

ANAIYA SOPHIA, MYSTIC, INITIATOR OF SACRED MARRIAGE,
AND AUTHOR OF *SACRED SEXUAL UNION*
AND *FIERCE FEMININE RISING*

"Reading this book felt like immersing myself in a bath of Mother Mary's light, opening up to remember again the holy womb and the timely miracle that filled me with renewed inspiration and hope. The description of the Mer priestess, her story, and her connection to the fae resonated deeply with me, reflecting much of what I've channeled and experienced in my own spiritual journey. These words beautifully capture the essence of the priestess path, reminding us that it is a deeply personal journey guided by love and divine calling. This book is a valuable contribution to the restoration of the light priestesses on Earth today."

ISHTARA ROSE, LIGHT PRACTITIONER, MEDIUM,
AND AUTHOR OF *MARY MAGDALENE*

"Compelling! More hidden Sacred Feminine mysteries coming to light as we move into the New Earth."

REENA KUMARASINGHAM, AUTHOR OF *SHROUDED TRUTH*
AND *THE MAGDALENE LINEAGE*

The Secret Life of
Mother Mary

Divine Feminine Power
for Personal Healing and
Planetary Awakening

Marguerite Mary Rigoglioso, Ph.D.

Bear & Company
Rochester, Vermont

Bear & Company
One Park Street
Rochester, Vermont 05767
www.BearandCompanyBooks.com

SUSTAINABLE FORESTRY INITIATIVE
Certified Sourcing
www.forests.org
SFI-00854

Text stock is SFI certified

Bear & Company is a division of Inner Traditions International

Cataloging-in-Publication Data for this title is available from the Library of Congress

ISBN 978-1-59143-524-2 (print)
ISBN 978-1-59143-525-9 (ebook)

Printed and bound in the United States by Lake Book Manufacturing, LLC
The text stock is SFI certified. The Sustainable Forestry Initiative® program promotes sustainable forest management.

10 9 8 7 6 5 4 3 2 1

Text design and layout by Kenleigh Manseau
This book was typeset in Garamond Premier Pro with Goudy OldStyle and Posterama Text used as Display

To send correspondence to the author of this book, mail a first-class letter to the author c/o Inner Traditions • Bear & Company, One Park Street, Rochester, VT 05767, and we will forward the communication, or contact the author directly at **sevensistersmysteryschool.com**.

Contents

To the Holy Marys ~ those love magicians ~
past, present, and future.

Acknowledgments

I deeply thank the following people who have inspired my path with Mother Mary:

My mother, Marie Dolores (Mary of the Sorrows), whose early departure from this world when I was a child served as an initiation for me to open to the reality of Divine Mother in her fullest manifestation.

Anne Yeomans, Patricia Reis, Prajna Halstrom, and Charlene Spretnak, for introducing me to a bold new Mary. Cavorting amidst a Goddess movement focused on exotic and foreign versions of the Sacred Feminine, their teachings revealed to me that the Goddess had been in my backyard the whole time in the form of a very familiar figure.

Lucia Chiavola Birnbaum, a strega nonna mentor, who helped me fall in love with the positive-valenced Black Madonna of Italy and Sicily.

Mary Beth Moser, for her touching devotion to the loving Black Madonna, which opened my eyes to what it would be like to love Mary in a personal way.

Patricia Anderson, for her unparalleled support and mentoring and her intuition that making this book interactive would serve readers in a far better way.

Claire Heartsong, for daring to serve as an oracle for the Holy Family and receive information that affirmed key aspects of what I was receiving intellectually about Mary.

Swami Sri Kaleshwar, for pulling the information about Mary and the Holy Womb Chakra from the ancient palm leaf manuscripts and for boldly sharing his recollections of her earth walk.

Cindy Lindsay, Sri Kaleshwar's senior student and a great teacher in her own right, who, in her course on the Holy Womb Chakra at the Divine Mother Center in Laytonville, California, shared these teachings as I sat with eyes brimming with tears of awe, feeling deep in my bones that truth was being spoken.

Den Poitras, a blessed male ally on the reality of divine birth who consolidated his knowledge in his very valuable book *Parthenogenesis: Women's Long-Lost Ability to Self-Conceive.*

Graelynn Corsini, Sidhe priestess, for inviting me to the Flying Lotus to present on my work on divine birth in Mt. Shasta in 2009 after my first book was published, for supporting the first workshop I did on divine birth for "re-membering" virgins and tantrikas, and for initiating me back into my Faerie lineage in Glastonbury that fine day by the trees.

Maureen Walton, who understood Mary's mystery through her knowledge of the divine birth of the Peacemaker of the Haudenosaunee people of New York and Ontario, Canada, and who encouraged me to teach about it at her Wyldwood Sojourn.

Christy Michaels, for inviting me to talk about my unique research on Mary for the first time publicly in 2009, and for continuing to invite me to speak about her and to co-create Mary and Magdalene ceremonies to bring healing and awareness to the community in the San Francisco Bay area.

Diana Marie Kelly, for affirming all of what I was receiving directly from Mother Mary, offering further helpful insights, encouraging me to work with this great being as a mentor, and modeling what that could look like in one's life.

Joy Reichard, Elizabeth Barton, Shannon Werner, and Catherine Ann Clemett, who keyed into my research on divine birth in 2009 and created a group in which we could continue the discoveries as holy women working together in meditation sessions.

Karen Holmes, for mystical teachings about the sacred weaver priestesses and other esoteric knowledge that further sparked my own inner knowing.

Amejo Amyot, for her encouragement of my Mary writing by housing me during my writing sabbatical in 2019, and for her own sharings of her relationship with Mother Mary.

My grandmother Elena Danisi Crimi Olsson, my Uncle Bob Crimi, and my Aunt Elizabeth Crimi Olsson, for their encouragement of me as a nonconventional "Virgin Mother," a woman with a penchant for the holy life whose children have been my writings and the many people who have granted me the privilege of being their teacher for a time.

Shannon Reich, for assisting me in sustaining Seven Sisters Mystery School as its executive assistant in its first eight years, for sharing her own passion for Mary (sometimes in the form of beautiful and rare prayer cards she has sent my way), and for introducing me to the wonderful book *Mary's Flowers*.

Roxy Runyan, my publicist, Karen Gordon, my administrative manager, and Courtney Harper, my former administrative assistant, for supporting me passionately in sharing my work with the world.

Tom Schneider, who knows why.

CHAPTER 1

Why Mother Mary Is Worth Rediscovering

I was lying in the hospital bed waiting for the surgery to remove the cyst on my left ovary to commence. But this wasn't the place I had been in a few moments earlier. Even though I was still listening to the same song streaming from Pandora into my ear buds, I thought. And, for some reason, I was burping.

As my mind came back to me things began to dawn. Was I in recovery? A nurse touched my arm. "You're in recovery; how ya doing?"

That's when I felt it, the wave. It was a wave of Mother Mary's love and energy, so strong that I almost couldn't contain it. I called the nurse over again. "I am feeling so much love, and I'm supposed to touch others and give it to them," I blathered, clutching her forearm.

"Well," she said with nursely tolerance, "people have all different kinds of responses" (she was referring to the ketamine in the anesthesia cocktail, I'd later find out), and she went back to her business.

All I could do was lie there radiating this great love to the entire room of awakening souls and their helpers as I looked at the clock and grappled with the eerie phenomenon of lost time.

Then I remembered: I had asked a group of six friends to take half-hour meditation shifts before, during, and after my surgery, and see me wrapped in a pink blanket of Mother Mary's love. I had forgotten. But here was that pink blanket, as big as the universe.

That day in November 2018 was my first palpable encounter with

1

Mother Mary after years of having been her dedicated researcher. It was the first of several miracle-ish type things that I was to experience in my decades-long relationship with this great female being. Because, finally, with a nine-centimeter fluid-filled sac on my ovary causing pelvic pain, she had coaxed me from my head into my womb—her favorite dwelling place.

It took me a long time to come around to Mary. Virgin Mary, Mother Mary, Mother of God, Blessed Mother—whatever people called her, for the first few decades of my life I wasn't very interested.

Can you blame me? Many modern women have trouble with the image of a female whose main attribute has been celibacy. A female whose perfection and purity are held as impossible models for behavior. A female who is obedient, docile, and deferring to all the males around her—including a god who decided that she was going to be The One without seeming to have gained her consent.

To my mind, getting too close to Mary carried the threat of having to give up all worldly joy and pleasures, enter a nunnery, and spend the rest of my life trapped in seclusion and prayer. At the very least it meant coming under pressure to be an eternal good girl with no sex life (certainly not before marriage) and very little in the way of anger. That didn't work for me, and I know it hasn't worked for many women, whether raised in Christian denominations or not.

Mary has not been sexy, and talking about her in any kind of devotional or honorific way has meant *you're* not sexy either. When a family guardian pressured me into taking *Mary* as my Catholic confirmation name, I was ashamed of having it. For years I didn't use it.

I want to help change this knee-jerk response to Mary on the part of many people. Over the past few decades, through my academic investigations and my own spiritual journey, I've come to know her in a new way. I've come to see her as a much more whole, integrated, and interesting being than the girl who has been portrayed in Christianity. Most people don't realize that Mary's identity has been cloaked, co-opted, and controlled and that this patriarchal maneuvering has greatly disempowered and disadvantaged all women . . . and all people. Just like that other great Mary we've come to re-know over the past several decades, Mary Magdalene, it's time for Mother Mary to be revealed too.

As I have shared what I've learned about the authentic Mary in lectures and conversations, many people, particularly women, have become intrigued, excited, and inspired. They have hungrily told me that they want to know more!

Through my scholarly rummaging and my direct experiences, I have come to know Mary as the greatest holy person who ever walked the planet. Not because she was a virgin—although she did spend at least some (if not all) of her life consolidating her sexual energies within herself. Not because she was perfect—although yes, she was a very advanced being. But because she modeled all that woman can be in her most evolved state: a fully embodied human on every level who completely manifested her Inner Divinity—what Plato and gnostic mystics sometimes referred to as the perfected Anthropos.

In the pages that follow, I will share the understanding I explored more fully in my previous book, *The Mystery Tradition of Miraculous Conception*—that Mary was first and foremost a lineage priestess of divine birth. That means she was born into a family and history of women who knew how to consciously conceive elevated beings as a means of helping humanity and planet Earth. These were women schooled in the mysteries of what the late Indian saint Sri Kaleshwar calls the Holy Womb Chakra. I will take you through my exciting discoveries that Mary was one of several powerful priestesses in her family and ancestry who had command over the human conception process and that she was part of a worldwide network of women who knew—and perhaps still know—how to carry out this practice.

I will also share how Mary, who in the New Testament basically drops out of sight after the birth of Jesus, also had a ministry that continued throughout her life. By exploring various revelations of the largely ignored histories about her, I will uncloak fascinating information about the teaching and healing ministry she passionately embarked upon, which focused on helping people cultivate love, compassion, for-giveness, personal empowerment, and healing capacities. This will lead us to understand who she truly was as a holy avatar, an incarnation of the Divine in human form. Yes, I have learned from the old manuscripts that Mary, herself, and not just her son, was a specially conceived being and that, as such, she was the living carrier of something much-needed in our world: Divine Feminine Wisdom.

In short I want to help people open to a fuller vision of Mary—and therefore new ways of being in relationship with her. Because what I have come to understand is that Mary is *available*. Due to her own tremendous spiritual achievements, she has become a resource on the inner planes that anyone (whatever your identity, religious affiliation, or level of spiritual interest) may draw upon to re-conceive, re-gestate, re-mother, and heal themselves.

She is also there to serve as a your "mentor" if you wish to move into your fully wise, fully advanced spiritual manifestation on earth. As we will see, she has always had a soft spot for and a special devotion to women, in particular—those who were alive while she walked the planet, and those still coping with patriarchy today.

One might say that Mary is available to help us move into the fifth dimensional consciousness that so many people are talking about now. This refers to a consciousness in which we are fully integrated in the material world while also accessing ever-deeper realms of know-ing. A consciousness that incorporates a soulful Sacred Heart of com-passion and love. A consciousness in which all of the energy centers of the human body, from root to crown, are operating at 100 percent capacity.

What follows is a far more comprehensive and compelling under-standing of Mary than we have seen in recent centuries. Through my intuition-infused academic research, I offer intriguing mystical possibil-ities surrounding what has been written about her life as a holy priestess of divine birth, a healer and spiritual teacher, and a woman who accom-plished the ultimate human achievement: transforming into divinity at the end of her earth walk—also known as *apotheosis*, or what is more commonly called "ascension."

My ultimate intention is to help you learn more about this "whole" Mary so that you can *experience* her yourself, either for the first time or more deeply than you ever have before. A relationship with the Goddess known as Mary can transform your life—and it can render you a minister of great healing and spiritual advancement on the planet.

Mary as a role model indeed offers a holographic imprint—not so much of perfection, but of possibility. What I receive from her is that in attuning to her essence we are actually awakening to *who we already are*. Thus she is ultimately but a mirror for our own divine beingness.

In this book are also some fascinating esoteric teachings about Mother Mary collected from others, as well as intuitive insights I have received while in expanded states of consciousness. I explore Mary's connection with the subtle angelic beings of the natural world. I share personal experiences I have had communicating with Mary in meditations, asking for help and healing. And I offer writing prompts and access to special guided journeys to help you engage with her more deeply. These tools will assist you in having a lived experience of this Great Master as a personal healer, a Perfect Mother, and a custom-made mentor.

THE MARY AND MAGDALENE PARTNERSHIP

As I mentioned earlier, over the past few decades another Mary, Mary Magdalene, has emerged from the shadows. New scholarly and intuitive understandings have led us to see her not as a prostitute, but as a holy woman who incorporated sexuality into her ministry. I have come to understand that both she and the Blessed Mother have been working in tandem to help humans restore women to their rightful and needed place. I believe that their illuminated advent in this age has been carefully timed and calibrated for the NOW.

I also sense that it was easier for these great masters to awaken the planet to their Sacred Female reality by having the seemingly sexier one go first. That is why this awakening to the Sacred Feminine aspect of the mysteries held within esoteric Christianity began with Magdalene. Numerous authors and spiritual teachers have introduced us to Mary Magdalene's true nature, history, and power, and thousands of people across the world have begun working with her on the inner dimensions.* Perhaps you are one of them.

Now that we have been shown the model of an integrated woman who is both sensual and spiritual, the door is open for us to take a new look at Mother Mary. In *The Mystery Tradition of Miraculous Conception,* I showed that she, too, has always possessed a sexual energy, one that has been fully integrated to fuel her service to humanity. Indeed it would have been impossible for a woman to self-conceive a child without also having a deeply alive erotic womb.

Thus we can now understand Mother Mary to be a passionate Sacred Feminine emanation, in every sense, along with the Magdalene. The Blessed Mother's "passion" has to do with not just her own suffering during the torture and murder of her son, as the word is commonly used in Christian parlance. It also relates to her love of others, her desire to bring healing to humanity, her care for planet Earth, and the fire of her own sensuality and sexuality.

This book will open new byroads on the pathway of reconnection with what these Marys ultimately represent: the Divine Creator herself. For as I understand it, and as we will explore in what follows, these two great female beings are holographic representations of the Great Goddess Sophia, whom I have also come to know as Mother Divine. They are members of a priestesshood that has been alive in every culture on the planet. For many, the Marys simply open the door to Goddess for millions who would not otherwise have gone there.

Women readers may come to understand that, like the Marys, you,

---

*Those wishing to experience Magdalene in this way may be interested in the on-demand course The Seven Mysteries of Magdalene, which can be found online at Seven Sisters Mystery School.

too, are a holographic representation of the Goddess. Other readers may find a new understanding of the feminine face of God, the inspiration to activate within you the yin qualities that will bring greater peace and nurturance to your lives and our world, and a loving unconditional mother and model for your own specific needs.

THE MULTIPLE MARY REALITIES

In my meditations I have received this message: it is important for me to remind you that the Mary I am sharing in this book may not look like your mother's Mary. She may not even look like *your* Mary, or anyone else's. And that is okay. I do not claim to have the absolute full picture of her. Your Mary is as valid as mine, and you may be tuning in to additional parts of her that can be brought to this great collective reconstruction of her, as well. Let's start a massive Mary movement!

There are also Marys who represent the rainbow of cultures and ethnicity. There are black Madonnas, brown Madonnas, white Madonnas, and more. Each one has her particular flavor, mission, ministry, story, and people. Maybe you gravitate toward one more than the other. That is wonderful, because each Mary brings her special gifts and her special medicine.

It is also important to recognize that there are a variety of stories and timelines about the events of and people in Mary's life. Some come from the New Testament. Some are found in the suppressed "apocryphal" or "gnostic" documents that were officially rejected by the Roman Catholic Church but that contain information that was held as gospel by people for centuries. Some stories and timelines have been presented to us from the meditations and flashes of insight of intuitive seers. Some of these stories are similar, some overlap, some are different or even contradict one another.

In this book I approach these stories with the idea that *all* of them are valid. The important point here is that various details, stories, or event timelines (a.k.a. "histories") will appeal to you based on the soul lessons that *you* need to experience. I encourage you to hold Mary's various histories and the people who espouse them with this perspective as well. With this approach, we do not have to argue over which Mary is "true" or "real" and create further division among us. We can accept that there are, in fact, as many Marys as there are people who think about her, and we can have an attitude of love and acceptance for everyone and their views. I invite the same of you, dear reader, as you consider the parallel histories about Mary that I have presented in *The Mystery Tradition of Miraculous Conception* and in this book.

Such tolerance is about more than "putting up with" others' views or "being nice" for the sake of maintaining peace and harmony. It is based on a deep esoteric insight that has been emerging for me with greater and greater insistence: the possibility that there are multiple realities. I have been persuaded to believe that there is no one truth, no one history, no one timeline of events. There is no one reality. There are many overlapping realities that can be grasped, held, tuned into—or even co-created—at any given time. All of them can exist simultaneously, even while people appear to be walking around in the same three-dimensional space. The factors that influence which reality you will embrace have to do with your beliefs about what is true, what is real, and what is possible. In other words, your reality is governed by your *beliefs* about reality. Those beliefs can shift at any time with new insights and new information. And a new reality and timeline can spin off in your own experience of your Earth walk as a result.

MARY "SEEING" AS
ADVANCED SPIRITUAL INITIATION

To further explore the mystical truth about the multiple nature of reality as regards Mary, and what this means for us, I present a telling segment of the Gospel of Philip. This is one of those writings about the teachings of Jesus dating from the second to fourth centuries CE, considered "heretical" by the Roman Catholic Church, and sometimes referred to as "gnostic." Although rejected by the official decision makers as valid documents, these texts contain what many consider to be the deepest of esoteric wisdom and truths. The Gospel of Philip says the following remarkable things about how Jesus appears differently to different people, depending on their level of consciousness. I invite you to substitute the word "Mary" for the word "Jesus," for the principle being described applies to her, as well:

> Jesus [Mary] tricked everyone. [S]he did not appear as [s]he was
> but in a way not to be seen.
> Yet [s]he appeared to all of them.
> To the great [s]he appeared as great,
> to the small as small. To angels [s]he appeared as an angel,
> and to humans as a human.
> And [s]he hid his [her] word from everyone.
> Some looked at him [her] and thought they saw themselves.
> When before his [her] students [s]he appeared gloriously
> on the mountain, [s]he was not small.
> No, [s]he became great and [s]he made his [her] students grow
> so they would know his [her] immensity.[1]

This gospel also tells us that by learning how to perceive in deeper ways, we can expand our consciousness:

> It is impossible to see anything in the real realm
> Unless you become it.
> Not so in the world. You see the sun without being the sun,
> see sky and earth but are not them.
> This is the truth of the world.
> In the other truth you are what you see.
> If you see spirit, you are spirit.
> If you look at the anointed, you are the anointed.
> If you see the father, you will be the father.

In this world you see everything but yourself,

but there, you look at yourself and are what you see.[2]

What these two passages are talking about is the fact that we see the great masters such as Jesus and Mary according to our *present* take on reality and our level of spiritual advancement. This means that if we are accustomed to being "small," then we are likely to see Mary as being little more than a pious and obedient girl. And, correspondingly, if this is the light we hold her in, it's the light we hold ourselves in. So in order to "see" Mary as the Great Master that I described earlier, we may need to become "greater" within ourselves.

In other words, again, reality is in the eye of the beholder. So if there is no real and true objective Mary "out there," that opens us to be able to ask, which Mary do we *want* to see/be?

These excerpts show us that "being" great and "seeing" greatness operate like a figure 8. When we penetrate beyond the illusions of the three-dimensional world into the "real realm," that is, the realm of Spirit, we experience nothing less than a great initiation. When we are able to truly "see Spirit," we become Spirit. When we are able to truly "see Christ," we become Christ. By seeing bigger and bigger versions of ourselves, we see bigger and bigger versions of the Masters.

I will boldly state: this book invites you to see that bigger version of Mary. It invites you to let Mary "make you grow," so that you may not only see Mary as Master, but, through this very seeing, know your *own* immensity and *become the Master yourself.*

I believe that this path of personal ascension (or IN-scension, as I prefer to call it, because spiritual deepening is an inner or inward process) is Mary's ultimate promise. What I have been shown is that she is not here just to heal you, and she is certainly not here just to be admired. She is here to help you manifest what has been called by some your "true divine nature" or your "Divine Human Blueprint." Yes, she is here to help you personally, and humanity collectively, to move into an entirely new dimension of being and become that exalted Anthropos.

This is the realm of what many are calling the New Earth, the domain of elevated living in which fifth dimensional consciousness is the order of the day.

Always remember the mantra for this book is: "Take what resonates, and set aside the rest for now."

Whatever your identity, whatever your creed, may this book help you fully embody within yourself GODDESS, She who is in co-creative evolution in service to her own growth and our earth and cosmos. Your whole, awakened self and your inspired action are needed right now as we face the next era of challenge and possibility.

HOW TO USE THIS BOOK

Looking at the Blessed Mother's processes and practices, many of which have been written about in this book, can give us insights and guidance as to how we may accelerate our awakening process. In order to partake deeply of what this book offers, I recommend that you purchase a beautiful journal. Or you may want to consider creating one yourself—either the entire book or just the cover (there are various short courses available on the art of book binding). Consecrate it as your own "Mary Journal" through a simple intention or ceremony. Then engage in the "Integration Activities" at the end of each chapter.

Whether you work with a journal or not, the information from this book will come truly alive for you when you use the guided audio meditations I offer at the end of each chapter. (See page 150 for information on accessing the free meditations.) These are a further means of helping you access powerful processes connected with Mary that have come through me. No doubt you will cultivate your own processes, as well, but these are a great start. You may also want to go deeper into the meditation process by spending some time writing about your experiences in your Mary Journal.

And please say hello to our community of those awakening to the higher frequency of Mary on the Seven Sisters Mystery School Facebook page (see page 151 for more on accessing the Facebook community). There you can share reflections and revelations from your work with the integration activities and guided meditations along with other comments about this book and your experiences working with this material. In this way we inspire one another and integrate Mother Mary's elevated presence into our lives and onto our planet.

CHAPTER I INTEGRATION ACTIVITY
Who Mary Is to You

Spend a few minutes reflecting on who Mary is to you at this moment. You may want to write this down in your Mary Journal. Or just hold it all within your heart.

- What do you know or not know about her?
- What does she mean or not mean to you?
- How do you feel about her? Passionate? Curious? Neutral? Ambivalent? Negative? Why?

.... Online Guided Meditation ....
Mother Mary as Midwife:
Rebirthing Your Inner Divine Child

In this journey, you will experience a powerful visualization in which Mother Mary will help you midwife the birth of your own divine self. You will enter the space in which the cleansing feminine fires remind you of your own holiness and the power you hold as a sacred being of the highest light. You will be guided to see yourself moving forward as this newly born being, fully protected and held by Mary and her own divinely born son, Yeshua—the Prince of Peace. See page 150 to register for the free meditations.

CHAPTER 2

Mary's Remothering of Me

It was a hot summer night in late July 1972, a few weeks after I had turned ten. My mother, Marie Dolores—Mary of the Sorrows—had returned from a two-week vacation with my father in Montauk, Long Island, but she hardly looked at me. She was too busy coughing, hacking endlessly on the fraying wicker furniture in my maternal grandparents' summer cottage in Lake Carmel, New York. The autoimmune disease lupus that had been slowly eating away at her body for years had gotten worse, much worse, since she'd been away.

"I'm dying!" she blurted out during one particularly strong fit, the way people do when they don't really mean it. But when my parents went home to Westchester that night, leaving my two younger brothers and me to spend one more night in the country, I locked myself in the bathroom for a long, long time, my body shaking. The next day my mother went into the hospital.

Two weeks later on August 11, my eight-year-old brother, Mark, and I sat quietly in the dark corner of the chilly basement apartment where my father's parents lived. We had spent many afternoons there during the previous two weeks while my father and other relatives visited my mother in the hospital; our two-and-a-half-year-old brother, Ray, stayed with neighbors. That day was different: my family members were late coming back. Very late. Finally the telephone rang. Grandma Lucia answered, spoke in Sicilian, hung up. "Mommy had a *hot etteck*," she said in her thick accent.

Heart attack? Heart attack? I screamed inwardly, my bowels turning to ice. Isn't that something for old men?

My grandmother looked at us futilely, wrung her hands, and shuffled into the kitchen. Mark and I remained seated opposite each other, divided by the heavy dining room table, bargaining with God against the unspeakable as we waited in silence.

Minutes passed. Hours. Ten thousand years. At last, the telephone blurted again. Mark and I started, our heads swiveling in synchrony as we watched our grandmother answer the phone. "Sì. Sì," she muttered. She turned toward us, the receiver suspended in midair, and uttered out loud what we immediately understood, despite her broken English: "*The worse.*"

The freefall began. My brother and I strained toward each other with outstretched arms. As we clasped one another, plummeting into blackness together, great animal howls were wrenched from our little bodies and sent forth into the universe.

MY SPIRITUAL AWAKENING

My mother's crossing served as an initiation into the realms of Spirit, Death, and the Dark Mysteries for me. Those mysteries had to do with the teachers known as Suffering, Karma, Duality, and Shadow, and how they relate to, and must be integrated with, the realms of Light. As I see it, I had been set upon a path to heal my soul from lifetimes of wounds and transgressions. This path was, it took me decades to understand, ultimately an initiation into *Sophia*, Divine Feminine Wisdom.

I am thankful for whatever blessings and privileges this road has included, but it has been filled with its share of . . . let's call them challenges. The years after my mother's death were a kind of hell-realm of abuse and neglect, which left me vulnerable and in need of love, guidance, and a sense of belonging.

As a child I already had mystical tendencies. Despite what to me was the general dreariness of the Catholic Mass, I tried to mine the gospel readings and dead homilies being offered for glints of gold. I found myself particularly stirred when Mary Magdalene would come into the picture at Easter time. The New Testament story frequently attributed to be about her—in which she anointed Jesus's feet with myrrh, wept, and wiped her tears with her hair—moved me deeply. It did not escape me that it was women who stood at the foot of the cross. And having lost someone too close to me for words, I could imagine I had at least a slight insight into what they were going through as they watched this traumatic event unfold before them in excruciating living color.

When I was seventeen and entered Vassar College, I dutifully continued to attend Catholic Mass throughout my freshman year, but I soon decided it offered little that was relevant to my life except for the artistic uplift I got from singing in a three-women folk group. That wasn't enough to keep me there. After I moved to the Boston area in my early 20s, I was drawn to a group that seemed more connected with the "essentials" of Christianity. Or, I should say, I was hooked into the group by a well-meaning person in my life who had also been hooked. By divine grace—namely a large newspaper expose that came out shortly afterward—we realized after just a few months that the organization was a fundamentalist cult.

Plunged into great inner turmoil, I scraped up the resolve to say goodbye to this group and worked with a cult exit counsellor to deal with the shock and shame of having been taken in like that. What chagrined me the most was the ease with which I had become a doctrine-spouting recruiter myself. Years later I understood that the experience had taught me some level of discernment, which would prove to be necessary in the esoteric and nonconventional spiritual waters I would increasingly swim in. It also taught me to be more careful with my gift of persuasion.

Shortly after the cult experience, as a kind of balancing corrective on the part of the universe, a friend gave me the book *The Politics of Women's Spirituality,* edited by Charlene Spretnak. I did not know then that Charlene would become one of my "Mary mentors" more than a decade later. All I knew was that the essays exposed the patriarchal abuses I had suffered as a woman—which had been particularly evident in the cult I had just left. They also showed me the intriguing possibility of a feminine-oriented spirituality based in honoring the Sacred Feminine and including women's needs and values.

For me these writings by women spiritual pioneers—many of whom would later become colleagues—were so potent that I could barely get through a page or two at a time. I knew at some deep level that I was breaking taboos by merely having the book in my hand. Goddess worship, for god's sake? Didn't that break all sorts of commandments and even have a scent of evildoing about it? I did not have adequate supports at the time for dealing with the emotions that were being triggered both by the material and the position of renegade it was thrusting me into, and I had to put it down.

The impetus of my spiritual drive couldn't be stopped, though. As the months passed, a friend turned me on to Jane Roberts and Sanaya Roman, and I soon became insatiably drawn to their information and the method by which they received it—namely, channeling, a form of direct revelation. Their work exposed to me to new dimensions of reality (and inspired me eventually to become a channeler—or what I prefer to call "an oracle"—as well as to teach others how to do it). On the heels of these discoveries I began to devour spiritual courses in the Cambridge, Massachusetts, area offered by a then-thriving (but now defunct) organization called the Interface Foundation, whose lectures and programs provided me with a safe entry into the world of the Sacred Feminine that I had glimpsed in Charlene's book.

I soon learned of several spiritual pilgrimages in Greece and Sicily, as well, and through these trips I experienced ecstatic personal encounters with ancient feminine mysteries in modern garb on power spots of great spiritual significance. This cavorting with women in open ceremony helped me fully break through the "taboo threshold," and I began to eat, sleep, breathe, and dream all things Goddess. I learned about the work of archaeologist Marija Gimbutas, whose writings affirmed the existence of the veneration of the Sacred Feminine at the earliest levels of old European civilization. All of this felt incredibly new—and yet like a great truth I had always known.

When I heard about an exhilarating "women's spirituality" program sponsored by Interface and led by Anne Yeomans, Patricia Reis, and Prajna Halstrom, I eagerly signed up. That program, and its offshoots, which lasted several years, invited many of the prominent explorers and pioneers in the new field of feminine spirituality to teach us about a wealth of topics near to my heart. It also helped me integrate my learnings through profound rituals of healing and spiritual initiation.

One of the areas of focus was on Mother Mary as a "goddess." Mary as Goddess? Now we were talking. The door began opening for me to an entirely new way of understanding the main female figure of the religion I had rejected.

During that period I took a goddess pilgrimage to Sicily to explore how the veneration of older Greek goddesses whom I had also come to love, like Demeter and Persephone, had morphed into devotion to Mother Mary. Three of my four grandparents were from Sicily, so this linking of my ancestry, my esoteric spiritual passions, and the Christianity I had been brought up with was deeply meaningful. Walking in street processions of the Blessed Mother at Easter time was a particularly moving experience that led me to feel as though I was connecting with ancestral feminine power at its most primal and potent level.

Meanwhile there was my "day job" as a staff writer at Harvard University and a part-time freelance writer. I began the process of uniting my two worlds as writer and soul journeyer by crafting a lengthy research article on the women's spirituality movement for a prominent spiritual magazine at the time called *New Age Journal*. Entitled "Awakening to the Goddess," the article marked my own start as a voice in this emerging field.[1]

MARY IN ACADEMIA

My hunger to learn much more and bring the Sacred Feminine to life led me to enroll as a graduate student at the California Institute of

Integral Studies (CIIS) in 1999. Over the next eight years, I happily earned my master's and doctoral degrees in philosophy, religion, and humanities, with a focus on women's spirituality—a specialty field of which CIIS was on the leading edge.

This is where I met Charlene Spretnak, who happened to be teaching a pioneering course on Mother Mary at the time that was based on the impressive research for her book *Missing Mary: The Queen of Heaven and Her Re-Emergence in the Modern Church*. Charlene stood as a model to me of an intellectual giant who also had a personal devotion to Mary. She showed me that, yes, a woman could be smart and Marianly spiritual, and that, in fact, the two could complement each other. At the end of the course, I gifted her with something every Mary afficionado needs—a Mother Mary nightlight, which she accepted with great delight and says still lights up her bathroom during the dark hours.

Charlene wasn't the only woman I admired at CIIS who loved Mary. There was also the late Lucia Chiavola Birnbaum, a renegade from the University of California at Berkeley and author of *Black Madonnas: Women, Religion, and Politics in Italy*. Her influence allowed me to embrace an "Italian" Mary to my heart's content—and to understand that the Blessed Mother's looks and languages truly span the globe. The late Mara Keller, then head of the women's spirituality program at CIIS, had me with her pioneering work on Demeter and Persephone.

I was inspired by all of these influences to write papers and a master's thesis on goddesses and priestesses of the ancient Mediterranean world. My research took me deep into the past and onto the ground at archeological sites in Europe. After earning my master's in 2001, with a thesis on Demeter and Persephone's ancient veneration in Sicily, I began spinning my research into courses in as many colleges, universities, and graduate schools in the San Francisco Bay Area as I could.

Meanwhile I began my doctoral work, which was leading me to something I had not seen coming—the discovery that certain holy women of antiquity had engaged in divine conception as a bona fide spiritual practice. Yes, starting with a bolt of inner insight and proceeding with cartloads of research books, I realized that divine birth was real, that Mary had literally accomplished it, and that the practice went far beyond her. I delved into the writing of my dissertation on the subject, and although I intended to include material on Mary, the writing on ancient Greece alone was ballooning into 600 double-spaced pages, so I had to lay her aside for the future. I turned that voluminous manuscript into my first two published books, *The Cult of Divine Birth in Ancient Greece* in 2009, and *Virgin Mother Goddesses of Antiquity* on the heels of that in 2010.

Right around that time I was led by accident to Claire Heartsong's book *Anna, Grandmother of Jesus.* I say "by accident" because I thought this was the book a friend had recommended to me. It turned out, however, that she had recommended another book entirely. My friend and I puzzled over this because somehow I found myself ordering Claire's book instead, which is a narrative based on direct revelations she received about the Holy Family while working in meditative states of consciousness. Clearly I was meant to connect with this work.

The timing was fascinating. Claire had published her book in 2002, shortly after I had begun receiving my intuitions about the reality of divine birth. So when I cracked open Claire's book in 2010 and saw that it contained information validating my own intuitive understanding of both Mary and her mother Anne as conscious priestesses of divine conception, I was gratefully astounded. It felt like an affirmation of what I had been receiving and a powerful message that the time for the unveiling of this information indeed had come.

I soon reached out to Claire and spoke with her by phone, explaining how our work seemed to converge. She emphasized one detail about both Anne's and Mary's miraculous pregnancies: "These were 'light conceptions,'" she said, pronouncing the words very carefully and deliberately. "Light conceptions" hit me right between the eyes because I knew from my research in ancient Egypt and Greece that divine birth was considered to be brought about by a "flash of light" from the heavens.[2] Claire's words bolstered the sense that she and I were working with the help of some kind of guided hand. They also led me to ponder at a deeper level the aspects of quantum physics that Mary and all divine birth priestesses were working with in their conception rituals.

For years I continued to spin out university courses one after the other, some of which included my research on divine birth and my "leftover" material on Mary's part in it. Although I had my sights on a professorial career, I eventually realized that there was no real room in the narrow halls of academe for a spiritual and scholarly maverick who wove together the intellectual with the intuitional. When I met a coaching mentor in 2012 who showed me how I could craft a living in a new, more inspired way, I realized I could just up and create my *own* teaching enterprise. With that, Seven Sisters Mystery School was born. This allowed me to integrate my academic material with experiential processes and practices I developed to help people, mainly women, cultivate themselves as evolutionary spiritual forces on the planet.

MARY, CAN YOU MOTHER ME?

This brief sketch skims over one important thing: the undercurrent of unresolved trauma in my life.

As my spiritual clock moved to seven, to eight, to nine, to ten o'clock, emotionally I stayed stuck at something like six. In other words, my growing intellectual and spiritual understandings were getting increasingly out of sync with a pain body that was crying for healing. On top of this, being a spiritual pioneer who was teaching about things that were beyond the scope of what was considered "real" by most people was creating an additional level of stress.

Over the years I had developed the capacity to consult with subtle intelligences through my explorations both in meditation and sacred medicine. I had been asking for and receiving help, guidance, and even healing. I had become my own version of an oracle and was teaching women how to serve in a similar way. But I just got to a place. A place.

The place where I needed to look at Mary as more than just a topic of research. I needed to explore in a personal way the aspect of her incorporated in this one word: Mother.

Yes, I held the reality that Mary walked the planet. I held the reality that she divinely conceived Jesus. I knew that she had many titles attesting to her attributes as a conduit of forgiveness and compassion. But I was so entrenched in the unappealing culturally held view of her that I just couldn't truly feel her as a source of nurturance and empowerment. I had already embraced the emerging understanding of Magdalene's original role as the head of the apostles and the beloved of Jesus, and I had been working with her inwardly (and teaching about her) for more than two decades. But Mother Mary? No.

That began to shift as I kept digging deeper into Mary's role in divine birth. I realized that if I was so drawn to the Magdalene, and if I could speak with the gods and goddesses of the ancient Egyptian and Greek pantheons, why not the goddess in my own backyard: Mary?

I was perhaps most strikingly given permission to look at Mary in a more profound way when I attended the Holy Womb Chakra System course offered by Cindy Lindsay through the Divine Mother Center in Laytonville, California, in July 2017. On the fourth day of that course, Cindy shared with us something that had been taught to her by her teacher, the Indian saint Sri Kaleshwar: Mary was the greatest holy person who ever walked the planet. Not just the greatest holy *woman,* but the greatest holy master of all time, period. Given all I had already learned about Mary, my response to this was: TRUTH!

Cindy told us something that made total sense to me, that Mary was a master of the practices regarding what Kaleshwar called the Holy Womb Chakra, a chakra related to but separate from the second chakra commonly understood to be that of sexuality and creativity. According to Kaleshwar, Mary had worked esoterically with Jesus from the time he was living inside her body to help him become a very great master himself, something we will explore in chapter 4. As the group of us sat there listening to these words, my sister colleagues and I began weeping.

At last Mary, as the full priestess and goddess that she had always been, was being returned to us.

The one thing the teachings did not cover, surprisingly, was how Mary used the womb chakra practices to achieve a divine conception to begin with. But of course they didn't. I knew why: that was mystery knowledge to be filled in by women. And given my background on divine birth in the ancient Mediterranean world, I figured I was the one to start things off with the first round of this revelation, and that this work would be taken up by others in coming years.

In the months that followed, as my pain body and fragmented "inner children" continued to cry out loudly for relief, I focused on working with Mary personally. I realized that I could ask her to do nothing less than re-mother this girl who had experienced the trauma of mother loss.

My esoteric priestess friend Diana Marie Kelly affirmed for me that Mary could reconceive and re-gestate me in her womb. She could re-raise me as a child. She could re-guide me as an adolescent. As I explored these possibilities, I came to see that she could even hold me in her arms like an infant when I was choking with anxiety in the middle of the night. I realized that you're never too old to need mothering, and who among us doesn't need an infusion of this kind of tender loving care throughout our lives? In fact, what better spiritual being to call upon for this than the master of perfect mothering herself?

Yes, Mary held the valence of Perfect Mother. I wondered why I had not figured all of this out before. It was suddenly so obvious. I began sitting in meditation to receive her healing practices, using them myself and teaching them to others.

MY MOTHER MARY WOMB ENCOUNTERS

Meanwhile my own Holy Womb Chakra had long been in need of healing, along with my tender heart. I began developing fibroids in my uterus and that cyst on my left ovary right around the time I started researching divine birth, back in 2003. I had surgery to remove the cyst in November 2018, while still living in California. The experience of donning the blue hospital gown and being transported on a gurney put me in contact with unrecognized trauma I held about what my mother's last days on earth must have been like in the hospital, and the fears that must have arisen within her as her body continued to deteriorate and she lost her grip on life.

My first Mary miracle, which I described at the start of this book, was spurred by the advice in the wonderful book *Prepare for Surgery, Heal Faster* by the late Peggy Huddleston, a woman I had known when I lived in the Boston area. She recommended that at the time of the surgery you have a group of people offer a special prayer and visualization for you. As I explained earlier, I asked a circle of friends to visualize me being held by Mother Mary in a pink blanket of unconditional love throughout the surgery. This resulted in the very strong and real presence of Mary emerging for me in the recovery room.

In 2019 I left California and headed eastward by car, fully relocating to Massachusetts by that September. A strange mass appeared on that same ovary that fall as I was writing what became both this book and my previous book, *The Mystery Tradition of Miraculous Conception*. In the terrified days I spent around Christmas waiting for results of a blood test to rule out a possible life-threatening illness, I pondered why my own womb seemed under siege, what I was doing wrong, and how it was that I could be "taken out" when I was pouring my lifeblood into serving Mary.

The message I received was that I was not ill; Mother was just trying to get me to put my attention on my womb at long last. Although I had studied the Holy Womb Chakra teachings, I had not healed and elevated my own womb by activating the mantras (chants) and yantras (drawings) included in that system for myself—a system that Kaleshwar claimed Mary and Mary Magdalene themselves had used. My foray into the mysteries of the womb had up until that point still been something of an intellectual pursuit. I received the message that if I were going to speak and teach about the Blessed Mother and her Holy Womb practices in an authentic way, I would need to purify and uplift my womb and teach from that place. On December 26, 2019, I began activating the main mantra of the system, the "mula" mantra, which meant reciting it 108 times in a row every day.

The next day the blood test results came back normal, but there was still the mass on my ovary to deal with. The nurse midwife in my new gynecology office had felt it in my pelvic examination, and, to my great distress, she said I would probably have to have it surgically removed and "looked at." The ultrasound confirmed that it was there, about four centimeters in diameter—a little meteorite within. "Findings represent SIGNIFICANT," the radiologist's report read, words that scared me. The gynecologist to whom I was assigned ordered a second ultrasound to be done to take a better look, despite the fact that the radiologist had recommended an MRI. The ultrasound ended up being scheduled for February 10, 2020.

During the waiting period I began re-listening to the entire Holy Womb Chakra course that I had taken with Cindy Lindsay in July 2017 and began listing what I needed to do to fully activate the mantras and get certified to teach the system. Meanwhile I continued to chant a full mala of mula mantras daily. I was also inspired to visualize, while chanting, the Blessed Mother's womb merging with mine and gently dissolving anything that did not need to be there. I asked her to heal me.

Then I forgot that I had asked.

In late January 2020 I had my monthly session with my own clairvoyant mentor Patricia Anderson. She saw distress in my pelvis that she could not calm down with her usual energetic techniques. "This usually means there's a physical problem," she said to me. I was totally terrified, especially given that in the five years I had been working with her I found that her seeing on all manner of things was quite often accurate, and as to any physical symptoms and associated fears I had, she had always reassured me.

I plunged into a hell of uncertainty and fear.

On Sunday, February 9, 2020, the Divine Mother Center, through which I had taken the womb class, included my name in their monthly fire puja ceremony. With the request, they ask for your intention in writing, so a month earlier on the online form I had stated "the dissolving of the mass on my ovary and the full healing of my womb." I watched the live two-hour fire ceremony lying down, as they instructed, listening to the lengthy chanting while holding my hands gently over my womb. I heard them call my name, crack a coconut open on a large rock in my honor, and sound the conch shell.

On February 10 the technician took the readings for my second ultrasound and then told me to stay on the gurney while she checked with the radiologist "to make sure he had all the information he needed." Was that a good sign or a bad one?

Two days later I sat for two hours in my new gynecologist's office, waiting to meet him for the follow-up. He was late due to some complications in a surgical case earlier in the day, so I sat on the table in the blue paper dress, with the computer on my lap, continuing to revisit the video lessons from Cindy Lindsay, which included special teachings about the power of the Blessed Mother's womb.

When the doctor finally arrived in the examination room, he seemed flustered and quickly scanned through the written documentation. He asked me for the history of my situation, and I briefly told him about the previous cystectomy. He finally said, "Well, the ultrasound showed nothing on your ovary."

I felt as though I was imploding and wanted to burst into tears, but I just kept my cool. Here I had been expecting to discuss surgery . . . but the mass was gone.

I asked if he wanted to palpate me just to make sure, and he said that yes, that was part of the plan. With a nurse in attendance, his big "man fingers" forcefully roved inside my vagina and outside on my belly, searching and searching. He could feel nothing.

I tried to explain that I had been doing "spiritual practices," but the words seemed to disappear into thin air. They registered neither with him nor the nurse. Eventually he asked, "Well, what was this practice? Group therapy?" I was too stunned by the whole experience even to laugh.

The doctor ordered an MRI, "just to rule out" anything. I agreed to do it, and this was seconded later by my clairvoyant guide Patricia, who said, "you need to document this miracle."

On March 2, 2020 just as the global health crisis was beginning to hit the United States, I lay in the MRI bed in the hospital, listening to the otherworldly sirens and groans being spewed by the magnetic forces circulating around my body. Three days later the gynecologist called to tell me that the MRI also revealed nothing on my ovary. Previously existing fibroids, yes. But no ovarian mass.

This was my Mother Mary Miracle number two.

The cycle was now complete. I understood that I had been led through this drama to have my own little in-house miracle attesting to both the power of Mother Mary and the womb chakra practices. I could now tell people with authority that yes, she heals, in co-creative partnership with YOU when you join forces with her in an active way.

MARY AS A REAL ESTATE AGENT

I continued to chant the entire cycle of eight Holy Womb Chakra mantras daily, 108 times, for 101 days. It was only months later that I realized that one week after I had completed "charging" the mantras like this, I finally found my new home, the first house I was to purchase in my life after three decades of renting.

I had been looking at properties for about a year and had seen about a hundred houses, most of which were "nos" and some of which slipped through my fingers in the bidding wars provoked by the economic strangeness and population migrations spurred by the health crisis in the summer of 2020. But on June 13 a sweet little house redolent of the Faeries popped up on the real estate listings for Berkshire County, Massachusetts. When I called the listing agent, he referred me directly to the owner, who was selling it privately. Although I was not able to reach her by phone, I noticed that the house right next door also happened to be for sale, and I contacted the realtor for that property, who agreed to let me in to both homes.

When I walked into the sweet Faerie house, my experience from the seemingly endless walk-throughs of other properties told me this place, built in 1949, had potential. The owner had clearly taken good care of it, and while it was small, there was the possibility of opening up a wall to create a more open space.

Then I noticed photos of three people, who turned out to be the owner's adult children, on the refrigerator. The kind realtor leading me through the house told me that one of them had died in his early thirties, struck dead by an oncoming car years ago when he was visiting Arizona and stopped to get cigarettes at a store. She showed me the urn with his ashes on a shelf in the center of the house.

The owner's office featured a shrine that included her son's photo on the wall, a Catholic prayer kneeler, and a small altar with images of Jesus and Mary. Among them was a prayer card of Jesus and Mary featuring their Sacred Hearts, identical to the one that I always took with me on my trips and that had been my constant companion in the place I was previously renting in the Berkshires.

The identical prayer card of Jesus and Mary that I always took with me.

It was such a stunning instance of alignment that it took me a moment to realize: Oh, my goodness, Mother Mary wants me to live in this house! Are you surprised to hear, dear reader, that the owner's name was Mary and that she indeed had a devotion to the Blessed Mother? I met her that afternoon, she agreed not to show the home to anyone else, and by Monday morning the contract was signed—at an incredibly economical price, in the midst of one of the most bizarre real estate markets we've ever known.

This was my Mother Mary Miracle number three.

I am grateful that I waited more than a decade to write my books about the Blessed Mother since beginning my journey with her because this time has allowed me to see and experience a whole new Mary several times over. I continue to be amazed by the image of her that has emerged even as I have been digging into her history and evolving my thoughts through the writing process and through the classes and circles I have offered on Mother Mary.* I am stunned by Mary's living power, which reached into my three-dimensional world to touch even my physical body. This work of the head, heart, and womb has enlivened my own spiritual journey with her.

There is so much information about this Great Master, this Great Mother, that is hidden away in the old texts as well as in more contemporary revelations. I am bursting with excitement at the thought of all that you are about to discover as we go forward.

CHAPTER 2 INTEGRATION ACTIVITY
Considering the Healing You Need

Reflect for a few minutes on the following questions. You may want to write your reflections in your Mary Journal.

- What is inside you wanting to be healed?
- How are you needing perfect mothering?

.... Online Guided Meditation ....
Receive & Embody Divine Maternal Nurturance: Healing Mother Wounds with Mary

In this inner journey with Blessed Mother as your guide, you will experience and absorb the whole mothering you may have never received. Feel the transformation as the light codes of nurture coming from this Goddess of Maternal Mastery work your body, mind, and spirit. See page 150 to register for the free meditations.

---

*These offerings are available online through Seven Sisters Mystery School, among them, the Holy Womb Chakra Teachings, the Monthly Mary & Magdalene Empowerments Circle, and new courses that will continue to be offered.

CHAPTER 3

Mary as a Conscious Priestess of Divine Birth

The first important thing to understand about Mother Mary's secret life is that she was not a passive vehicle to her conception of Jesus. According to my research she was an active, willing orchestrator of this great event. As I mentioned in chapter 1, Mary was, in fact, a trained priestess in a lineage of women who knew how to divinely conceive special holy children going back to the early days of the Hebrew tradition.

The purpose of the practice was to bring forth avatars—walking representations of the Divine who could not be born through "regular" means. The intention was for such offspring to serve as high-level leaders for humanity. This priestess role was not just the special gift of Hebrew family lines; it spanned the globe in many cultures. We hear the most about it as it relates to Mary, however, because she was a particularly high adept of this kind—which enabled her to usher an exceptionally extraordinary being onto our planet.

How do I know all this? To unveil Mary's suppressed history, I drew on evidence from my first two books, *The Cult of Divine Birth in Ancient Greece* and *Virgin Mother Goddesses of Antiquity*. This rare background qualified me to decode the secrets that Mary's forgotten gospel, the Infancy Gospel of James, has long hidden in plain sight. In my third book, *The Mystery Tradition of Miraculous Conception: Mary and the Lineage of Virgin Births*, I delve into that gospel, which was originally entitled Birth of Mary, to show how Mary was trained, and I reveal some of the esoteric techniques she used to conceive Jesus.

I offer a summary of that detailed work in this chapter, but if you want to understand Mary's history in its entirety with all of the references I have collected, I highly recommend that you read that book as well. Taken together both that book and the present volume provide a complete and up-to-the-minute account of this most holy of women. *The Mystery Tradition of Miraculous Conception* also provides important background on the history and practice of divine birth as a real activity of priestesses more broadly. This will help you understand Mary in the context of holy women's work spanning widely across ancient Europe, West Asia, and Northern Africa.

IT BEGINS WITH SARAH

To understand Mary as a divine birth priestess in a lineage of Hebrew women, we need to travel back in time to the biblical matriarch Sarah, the famous wife of Abraham. Many are familiar with the story of Sarah's miraculous birth of her son Isaac when she was in her elder years. But what most people don't realize is that first, Sarah was a significant holy woman in her own right, and second, there is much evidence suggesting she was trained in a tradition of divine birth that spanned West Asia.

Intriguingly Sarah's roles were remarkably similar to those of several types of priestesses in this area of the world roughly around time she would have lived. When we penetrate her history, we come to realize that she delivered prophecy, maintained celibacy, and even engaged in sacred marriage rituals. Yes, these rituals involved her embodying the Goddess with male gods, or perhaps male priest–kings, in sexual rites that were originally meant to bring forth divine children. As I show in *The Mystery Tradition of Miraculous Conception*, it is likely that Abraham was never her formal husband in the way we traditionally think of it. He was more of a sacred guardian, and Sarah may have engaged with him sexually only during these sexual rites, if at all.

Based on what I have uncovered in my research, these characteristics tell us that Sarah was nothing less than a priestess of divine birth. What we see, however, is that she was operating in a time in which the work of divine conception was being controlled by patriarchal religious leaders and laws. As I have discerned, Sarah's statement, "The Lord has kept me from having children" (Genesis 16:2), is not what we've been led to believe it is—a woeful lament about her biological barrenness. Instead, it refers to the religious law she was being pressured to follow that forbid her from becoming pregnant in sex rites.

What's more, it is likely that Abraham's famous attempt to sacrifice Isaac, whom Sarah eventually did successfully conceive through non-ordinary means, was an effort to obey this law and follow through with the horrific custom of killing any child that was conceived during a divine birth ritual. In short Sarah was a divine birth priestess with a desire for a child, and her womb was being restricted and controlled. She nevertheless persisted in her art until she was able to bring forth Isaac. Ultimately Abraham was divinely guided not to kill her child.

I found it fascinating to discover that Sarah wasn't the only Hebrew matriarch to serve in the role of divine birth priestess. This I learned about in the document known as "De Cherubim," written by a Hellenistic Jewish philosopher named Philo who lived in Alexandria, Egypt, approximately 20 BCE to 50 CE. Philo asserts that divine conceptions also took place for the other matriarchs: Zippora, the wife of Moses; Rebecca, the wife of Isaac; and Leah, the wife of Jacob.* This means that, far from being only a "Christian thing," divine birth was firmly embedded in the Hebrew tradition.

---

*See Philo, *De Cherubim* 12:40 onward. In another work (*De Mutatione Nominum*, 132–33), he adds Tamar to the list.

ANNE PICKS UP THE THREAD OF DIVINE CONCEPTION

We now leap forward in time to Anne, a sacred woman who is revealed in the Infancy Gospel of James/Birth of Mary to have conceived Mary through unusual means, just as Sarah did Isaac. Many of the details in Anne's story echo what we find in Sarah's story, which, I believe, links these two women through time as priestesses of miraculous conception.

What we learn in Mary's suppressed infancy gospel is that Anne and her companion Joachim were special holy people who held a very high status in their Jewish community. Anne conceived Mary without having sexual relations with Joachim through an elaborate ritual for which she was likely trained.

As we hear in the gospel, this rite began with Anne ritually cleansing herself. Based on what we know from ancient texts describing sacred marriage rituals of the kind for which she was probably readying herself, this may well have included washing her sacred vulva. Anne then donned her "wedding dress" as part of this ritual—a further sign that she was orchestrating a "sacred marriage" rite. But in her case, since Joachim was far away in the wilderness, we know that she was preparing for an "inner" sacred marriage to engender a kind of parthenogenesis, or true virgin birth. Anne's was not a rite to be enacted with a male being.

The location of Anne's ritual was important. Working with special timing, she situated herself in her sacred garden, the very kind of place known in the ancient world where the veils between the dimensions were considered to be thin—and therefore where prophecy and other non-ordinary things could take place. Anne was possibly assisted in her process by ingesting laurel, which opened her consciousness and allowed her to sense the presence of a divine messenger who was assisting her. She used prayer to call upon divine power, and she also invoked her ancestress, the biblical matriarch Sarah, for her help in this rite. This invocation linking the two women again shows us that they were part of a longstanding lineage practice.

Meanwhile Joachim had pitched himself out into the wilderness to conduct his own "vision quest" in which he would call on divine powers to help Anne in her challenging task. When Anne experienced the moment of "ego death," that is, the "rock bottom" point at which she felt lesser even than all living creatures who reproduce through regular means, she achieved the required state of humility, and the conception of her daughter was able to occur. A divine messenger appeared to her to affirm her success.

THE SACRED CODE WORD *MARIÁM*

After giving birth Anne graced her daughter with the name that has come down to us as *Mary*. The actual name at the time would have been *Maryam* or *Miriam*, which may well derive from the Egyptian word *MRY/Mery*. That Egyptian term meant "beloved of," "desired," "delight," "loving," "lover," and "the loving one." Thus the name *Maryam/Miriam/Mary* essentially meant "Beloved of the Divine" or "Divine Love." It was certainly a fitting moniker for a child who was not just an ordinary human, but rather, through her own unusual conception, an avatar.

Working in meditation I further received that the version of this name that appears fleetingly in Mary's infancy gospel, *Mariám*, contains specific seed syllables that serve as initiatory codes to unlock your own inner divinity when you utter it as a mantra. For in it, we find *Ma*, *Ri*, and *Am*.

Ma is the near universal linguistic marker for "mother," and *Am* can be seen as a form of *Aum,* that is, *Om*, the great Sanskrit seed syllable of universal creation, thought to consist of three sounds: *ah*, *oo*, and *mm*. It is uttered as a mantra and in affirmations and blessings. *Ri* can be understood as the word *hri*, a Buddhist term translated as "self-respect," "conscientiousness regarding one's actions," or "moral self-dignity."* In other words it can be seen to mean "self-love"!

---

*Tibetan Buddhist Encyclopedia contributors, "Hrī."

Putting these syllables together *Mariám* can be understood to mean "Mother of Impeccable and Self-Loving, Sovereign/Virgin Universal Creation." It contains the alpha—*Ma,* the Mother who creates—and the omega—the *Am/Aum,* the Creation itself. These are linked together through self-love/self-generated consciousness—*(H)ri.* The name is balanced, beginning and ending with the same letter, the first and last syllables mirroring one another. This gives it a flow, a back-and-forth quality, much like a figure eight, which to me suggests that it refers to both the white hole, which births universes, and the black hole, which absorbs them and births them out in a new white hole, in a constant rhythm of parthenogenetic, or virgin, creation.

Mariám can also be seen to contain within it *Mar I Am. Mar* comes from the Latin word "mare," or "sea." Mary was seen as the patron of sailors, and later came to be known as "Stella Maris," Star of the Sea. The Greek tradition equates "sea" with "universe" through the concept of Okeanos, the sea that surrounds the Earth and in fact contains the entire cosmos. In French the word is *Mer,* which comes closer to the Egyptian term *MRY/Mery,* again, the principle of Divine Love. We will recall that "I Am that which I Am" is the name of the Divine as told to the biblical Moses (Exodus 3:14).

So seen another way, *Mar I Am* or *Mer I Am* can similarly be understood to mean "I am the Divine Love Universe." Because it includes the feminine aspect of that universe, it is a corrective to the strictly masculine version of the name of God.*

Going further the name can be stretched to sound like *Mery I Am,* meaning, essentially, "Beloved I Am," or "Love I Am." When slightly stretched to sound like *Mary I Am,* this name can also be used as a mantra for merging yourself with Mary and, in that way, for self-initiating into her Sacred Order of the Marys—about which I will discuss more in the epilogue.

---

*I wish to acknowledge my colleagues Karen Holmes and Diana Marie Kelly, who have simultaneously also been working with Mary's name mantra, each in her own way.

Thus the word *Mariám* itself serves as its own powerful mantra for those who wish to invoke the tremendous creative and loving power of Mother Mary into their lives. The link to the audio I reference at the end of this chapter will allow you to play with all of these mantric possibilities so that you may explore all of this for yourself.

It's important to note that the Egyptian term *Meri/Mery*, again, from which the name *Maryam/Mary* was likely derived, was a sacred title that specifically connected its holder to the goddess Isis, the Great Mother who gave birth miraculously to her son Horus. The similarities between Mary and Isis are far more than coincidental. In fact scholar and spiritual seer Rudolph Steiner held that Mary was none other than Isis herself, reborn in a transfigured form.[1] The intriguing idea that Mary's lifetime on earth was not her first is something that the Hindu saint Sri Kaleshwar also maintained, as I will discuss in chapter 4.

Steiner also held that both Isis and Mary were emanations of Sophia, who is a form of the Great Goddess.[2] All of this means that, right at the start, Anne's choice of the name *Mary* identified her daughter as the ultimate expression of the Divine Feminine. I have come to the understanding that, like *Meri*, the term *Maryam/Mary* was originally not a personal name but, in fact, an honorific title. Although it came to be used as a personal name, it was mainly a *priestess title* for sacred women devoted to Divine Love and womb mysteries. This explains why we see so many *Mary*s running around in the New Testament. I contend they were all members of this holy order—something I will talk about more in chapter 5 when I discuss Mary Magdalene's role in this regard. Such naming by Anne thus served as a prophecy that her daughter would indeed carry out a massive role as an embodiment of the Great Mother who took womb magic to its ultimate fulfillment.

MARY'S CHILDHOOD TRAINING

The Infancy Gospel of James/Birth of Mary also fills in information about who Mary was and what her life was like before she conceived

Jesus, something we never hear about in the "official" canonical gospels. We learn that not only was she herself conceived through specialized means—which, again, rendered her a very high being in her own right—but also that she was trained as a divine birth priestess from the time she was six months old. Anne raised her in a bedroom sanctuary tended to by Hebrew temple virgins who began imparting to her various sacred practices that continued through her first few years of life.

As a sign of her holiness, Mary's feet were never allowed to touch the ground. She was fed a special diet, which may have included sacred medicines to open her consciousness, and she also practiced fasting. She was protected from impure influences of any kind, which allowed her to keep her emotions calm and her thoughts elevated.

The virgins took Mary through a process of "inner" cleansing, which may have included activities such as prayer, song, and specific rites not revealed by the gospel. This also purified her body so much that it probably did not need to menstruate when puberty hit. It seems that these virgins may well have taught Mary how to work with the "sacred sounds" or "tones" of the angelic realms as well, and that they also taught her sacred dance associated with this. I'll return to the theme of Mary's work with sound in chapter 4, when I discuss her probable use of sacred mantras—and their applicability to our own lives.

When Mary was three, Anne and Joachim made a great sacrifice: they had the virgins take her to live in the Hebrew temple with them. It was at that point that her formal education really began, with the virgins leading her through a series of further "purifications" and instruction in divine conception. Her training intensified with special food and possibly also sacred medicine to continue to expand her consciousness and prepare her to be a "dove"—that is, a priestess of divine birth. Mary was also eventually assigned a sacred male guardian, Joseph, whose role it was to look after her and support her for her mission to come.

What we understand from all of this is that Mary was a priestess who enjoyed a double empowerment. First she came to the planet already an avatar, a holy expression of the Divine Feminine, by virtue of her miraculous birth by Anne. Second she was given extensive training in order to take up the divine birth practice on her own. This unusual combination of pedigree and training enabled her to conceive a particularly powerful avatar of world service and transformation.

MARY'S CONCEPTION OF JESUS

Mary's infancy gospel tells us about her conception of Jesus in far greater detail than we find in the gospels of Matthew and Luke. What comes to light is a vision of Mary as part of a sisterhood of holy women of virgin birth in the Hebrew temple.

The metaphor her gospel uses to describe her miraculous conception process is that of the "weaving" of the great temple veil, the textile that was meant to guard the entry to the holy of holies. Mary was selected for that project—that is, this divine birth ritual—as part of a group of eight women who all hailed from the same exalted lineage. This cohort included Elizabeth, who, I discovered through research into the Islamic tradition, was likely to have been Mary's aunt. We see in the ritual that Elizabeth was also able to conceive a child divinely— her son John, who would come to master and use the water element in sacred ways in his own ministry and would become known as the "Baptist." All of this suggests that Mary was part of a specific bloodline of trained women, and that these women were all somehow working together in this remarkable ritual.

We can see that Mary was assisted in the process by first opening her awareness. She may well have accomplished this by drinking some kind of mind-expanding substance, which allowed her access to the inner domains of consciousness needed for her work. In her open state she, like her mother before her, was able to speak directly to a divine messenger, who was also critical in guiding the process.

The gospel tells us that Mary then engaged in an activity akin to "spinning and weaving," which I believe is a reference to energetic techniques she used to access the state necessary to achieve divine conception. This resulted in the generation of sexual, or kundalini, "heat" or "fire" in her womb, and its corresponding "light," which is a form of consciousness itself. As part of this work, she was simultaneously producing or tuning into some kind of sacred sound, word, or song of the universe. We'll return to her womb practices when we take a look at Sri Kaleshwar's teaching about this later on.

Mary's later title, "Stella Maris," "Star of the Sea," points to a mystical understanding that in her conception rite she was also working with the realms of light in the sense that she was connecting with Source Consciousness, perhaps in the form of "star beings." As I noted in chapter 2, Claire Heartsong has affirmed through her clairvoyant work that the divine pregnancies among Mary and the women of her lineage were "light" conceptions. All of this suggests that, for the conception process, Mary interacted with the light/matter interface at an exceedingly sophisticated level.

Mary's process was governed by a lack of ego and an abundance of love. For it is ultimately the love element that fuels the entire divine birth process and makes the conception possible. Mary's name/priestess title, which, as we have seen, means "Divine Love," was indeed a prophecy she fulfilled.

What is particularly noteworthy about Mary's conception of Jesus, in contrast to Anne's conception of Mary and the biblical Sarah's much earlier conception of Isaac, is the complete lack of involvement on the part of her companion, Joseph. While Anne was supported by Joachim energetically during his vision quest, and Sarah may have been involved in a physical sacred marriage rite with Abraham (or another male), we see no such parallel situation with Mary. The most we hear from her gospel is that she was made pregnant by the *logos*, or soul of the universe. I believe this is describing the complete solo engagement she had with divine powers to induce her pregnancy and that therefore her conception of Jesus was a case of pure, sovereign parthenogenesis. I propose that Mary was able to accomplish this huge feat by virtue of the fact that she was already a living incarnation of the Great Mother Goddess. This was the result both of her own divine birth and her purification practices. In other words Mary's specific process tells us that she was the most advanced of all the women who conceived miraculously before her.

Mary experienced a series of challenging events following the conception of Jesus. First she endured accusations that her pregnancy was the result of a sexual encounter that marked the breaking of her vow as a temple virgin. Then during her travels while pregnant, she experienced a remarkable prophetic vision predicting the agony and the ecstasy that Jesus's advent on the planet would stimulate on earth. Finally after birthing Jesus in a secluded cave, she became the target of King Herod's hunt to find and murder both Jesus and the divinely born John.

Meanwhile her aunt Elizabeth fled to safety in the mountains along with her son, John. Elizabeth's companion Zechariah steadfastly refused to reveal John's whereabouts and met a gruesome death at the hands of Herod's henchmen for his defiance. Mary's infancy gospel concludes with its author, James—who may have been the son of Joseph by a previous woman—telling us that he was forced to go into hiding during this dangerous period for the Holy Family, during which he penned the account of these events.

This exploration of Mary as a trained agent in divine conception is far different from the story Christianity has given us of a passive and bewildered girl who had little idea what was happening to her. It puts her in her rightful place, front and center in the story of Jesus. It shows us that Mary was a conscious actor who deliberately intended for Jesus to come into our world, and it restores her as the initiator and orchestrator of these significant events.

This chapter has started us off with the uncloaking of Mary by focusing especially on her powers of conception—powers that were not hers alone, but were and are capacities open to *all* women who wish to go deeper on their spiritual path. We will explore much more about Mary's womb mastery and what this tells us about her—as well as the promise it holds for all women.

CHAPTER 3 INTEGRATION ACTIVITY

Considering Divine Conception

I recommend you take up your Mary Journal and reflect on the following questions:

- What does the possibility that Mary conceived Jesus in a seemingly miraculous way stir within you?
- Does it make sense to you? Why or why not?
- Does it validate any thoughts you've had on your own? Stimulate any "memories"?

.... Online Guided Meditation ....

Chanting the Sacred Name of Mary

Join in this remarkable guided chant to experience and access the power of the sacred syllables encoded in the ancient name *Mariám*. As you do so, reflect on the meanings of *Ma, (H)ri*, and *A(u)m* as elucidated above in this chapter. Incorporate their resonances into your being so as to deepen your own relationship with the great Marys and support your spiritual awakening. See page 150 to register for the free meditations.

CHAPTER 4

The Power of Mary's Holy Womb Chakra—and Yours

Having begun the uncloaking of Mary by exploring her childhood and adolescence and the pieces often missing from her story, it is time to look further into who she was and what she offers us as a living presence today. For it is in this careful uncovering that a new, elevated Mary really begins to come alive and can be accessed as a healer, teacher, model, and guide for us in our own spiritual evolution and in our work to uplift humanity.

Various spiritual teachers over the last several hundred years have provided information about the Blessed Mother that they have received through direct revelation. Their insights attempt to fill in even what her suppressed "apocryphal" gospels leave out. Perhaps the most well-known among such individuals are Anne Catherine Emmerich, Rudolph Steiner, and, as I mentioned earlier, Claire Heartsong.

I will focus here on the teachings about Mother Mary that have been shared by the late Indian saint Sri Kaleshwar. One of the things I find so exciting about Kaleshwar's work is that it presents Mary (and Jesus) as having engaged in a living body of practices that come from a long, tried-and-true tradition. Because these practices have been carried out by holy people from time immemorial, their revelation in association with Mary helps us to understand her as a female mystic and saint—what is known in the Hindu tradition as a "Bhairavi Mata."

By grasping more of the practicalities of what Mary was up to in this role, we can comprehend her as real flesh-and-blood participant on her own spiritual path, rather than as a passive figure to whom inexplicable and weird things just seemed to "happen." We can strip away the haze of unbelievability from her story, and we can understand what she was doing on a technical and real level. As we look upon her from this more empowered place, we are simultaneously lifting ourselves up—a process of spiritual advancement revealed to us in the Gospel of Philip, as I discussed in chapter 1. What's more, Kaleshwar's information provides us with concrete tools and techniques that we can adopt for ourselves, thereby allowing us to literally follow Mary on the ascension/IN-scension path.

I also want to reiterate that what I present here is, in some of its details, an alternative to the traditional Mary history. Kaleshwar's information is esoteric but enhances what I spoke about in chapter 3 regarding her role as a divine birth priestess because it explains her sacred womb capacities from a grounded Hindu perspective. To me, what he says feels like the missing link so many of us have been waiting for. I leave it up to you as to whether this information feels like truth for *you*. Remember, take what resonates, and set aside the rest for now.

Who was Sri Kaleshwar? Although little is known about him outside of India and a small and growing group of spiritual practitioners who draw on his teachings, he was a highly regarded saint to whom various miracles were attributed. Born in India in 1973, he began his teaching and healing ministry in 1997, and left the earth plane in 2012 at thirty-nine years old.* His life was relatively short, but his influence continues on.

In his book *The Real Life and Teachings of Jesus Christ*, Kaleshwar reports that some of the information he teaches about Jesus and Mary comes from memories of his own past life with them when they walked the earth. However most of his teachings in this regard come from what

---

*This and other information about his life and teachings can be found on the Sri Kaleshwar Ashram and Sri Kaleshwar websites.

are known as the palm-leaf manuscripts of India, thousands of texts inscribed on dried palm leaves that preserve mantras (sacred chants), yantras (sacred diagrams), and other important spiritual and historical information, penned in languages including Sanskrit and Telegu.

According to Kaleshwar, the information on the palm leaves was originally written by seven ancient Indian sages known as the Saptarishis. Remarkably he says that the teachings conveyed on them were studied by Jesus, Buddha, Mother Mary, Mary Magdalene, and various other holy people of the past, who learned many important practices from them—and who even contributed writings to the palm leaves themselves.*

The Saptarishis are revered in Hinduism as the seven holy sages, and in the Vedas they are regarded as the founders of the Vedic tradition. They are considered to be enlightened beings who were "born from the mind" of the Hindu god Brahma. According to Hindu tradition, these special sages live for an enormous period of time known as a *manvantara* (306,720,000 earth years). They continue to exist through the cycle of creation and destruction of the universe, and work to uplift humankind and enlighten the planet to its full potential. At the end of a manvantara, when the universe is destroyed, the Saptarishis merge with the Divine. The task of guiding the earth is then given to newly appointed Saptarishis, who are believed to work closely with the Hindu god Shiva.† In this tradition, they are considered the most evolved "light beings" in creation, and the guardians of the divine laws.

---

*See Kaleshwar, *Real Life*, 35–58, for his own past life history with the Holy Family and information about the Indian palm leaf manuscripts. See also Monica of Penukonda, "The Divine Mission" and the "What Is in the Palm Leaf Manuscripts" section of the Monika of Penukonda website, where Monika writes, "The palm leaf manuscripts were revealed to the ancient rishis (sages) by the Divine Mother. They contain the body of knowledge that Jesus, Mary, and Mary Magdalen practiced."

†For more on the Saptarishis, see Wilkins, *Hindu Mythology*, 365, and Prakash, *Prashna Kundali and Saptarishis*.

What's important here is that in one version of an Indian legend, the Saptarishis are considered the seven central stars of Ursa Major, the Big Dipper. Their wives are the female beings who came to be known as the Krittikas, or the Pleiades. The Seven Sisters of the Pleiades have been known worldwide since antiquity as "seven starseed mothers" of the human race, female beings who birthed lineages on our planet and whose DNA runs through all of humanity.* Helena Blavatsky, the great seer and founder of Theosophy, affirms, "These Pleiades . . . have an interchange of thought with the Rishis."[1] This intimate esoteric relationship suggests to my mind that information from the Saptarishis about the Holy Womb Chakra may in fact be Pleiadian teachings. It certainly would be fitting that this information on the Holy Womb was in fact conveyed by female star beings who were practitioners of virgin birth.†

Whether you are open to this history of the Saptarishis and the Pleiades as "real" or not, I invite you to consider the information that I am about to share on its own terms. Does it speak to you? Does it ring as truth?

For me the palm leaf revelations from the Saptarishis that Kaleshwar relates about Mary and Jesus have sparked further understandings about these masters that I continue to take into my own heart, mind, and womb. As I mentioned in chapter 2, when I first learned some of what I am about to share from Cindy Lindsay's Holy Womb Chakra course, I was filled with a searing joy. After having embarked upon a decades-long sojourn to discover the Sacred Feminine and recover women's priestess power, I was deeply moved to find the essence of these things where they had been all along: in the

---

*See Rigoglioso, *Cult of Divine Birth*, 161–69, for an extended discussion of lore about the Pleiades in this regard.

†Cindy Lindsay, Sri Kaleshwar's senior student and my teacher, however, has noted in personal conversation with me that ultimately the teachings come directly from Mother Divine herself. Again, another senior student of Kaleshwar, Monika of Penukonda, affirms in the "What Is in the Palm Leaf Manuscripts" section of the Monika of Penukonda website, "The palm leaf manuscripts were revealed to the ancient rishis (sages) by the Divine Mother."

Christianity of my childhood. It had taken many years, many miles, and the words of a holy man from a non-Christian lineage, no less, for me to have this information fully returned to me. In receiving this potent downpour of revelations, I felt I was receiving one of the greatest healings I could experience as a woman. I also felt I was participating in the great healing of the feminine writ large.

KALESHWAR'S REVELATIONS ABOUT MARY

Sri Kaleshwar's message about the Blessed Mother can be boiled down to this: Mary was the closest-to-perfect human incarnation of the great goddess he called Mother Divine. *This rendered her the highest-level holy person who ever walked the planet, someone who possessed even greater power than her son, Jesus.*[2] Again, this means she embodies what has been referred to in gnostic sources as the exalted Anthropos, the fully perfected, fully realized human.*

To better understand Kaleshwar's portrayal of Mary, it is first important to look at what he says about Mother Divine (note that English was not his first language, so some of his phrases, which were not altered by his editors so as to preserve their authenticity, contain a unique charm):

Mother Divine is the Mother to every divine soul in this universe. She doesn't belong to any religion at all. The Mother is the universal God/Goddess. Period. She's an unbelievable vast ocean. You can't drink all of Her drops of water. You can digest some but not completely. Some is still left. That is She. Mother is the woman of huge love. She is also, same part, a woman of huge anger. One part is positive. One part is negative. In the Indian spiritual tradition, they

---

*See for example the Gospel of Mary [Magdalene], 10, where Mary Magdalene refers to this concept of the Anthropos as the perfected human, and King's commentary on this in *The Gospel of Mary of Magdala*, 59–62.

say she is the nature. In the nature, you can see very beautiful flowers and beautiful lakes. It is gorgeous. This same nature brings huge earthquakes, floods, and many disasters. Mother Divine's nature is like that. But once She starts to calm down, here you go; anything, whatever you want, you can receive from Her.

You should taste Her in both ways—then only you can really understand Her. Otherwise, there is no fragrance in your life. You didn't understand the real truth . . . You really only saw the material of life and only experienced the normal surface love. You didn't see the deeper, inner side of creation, up and down. . . .

The Divine Mother is the big Mother to take care of you. . . . Once you see Mother Divine, once you connect to Her, from that point, your real life will start in spirituality.[3]

With these statements Kaleshwar is first of all contributing significantly to the great work that has been taking place on the planet in recent decades to connect humanity with the Supreme Divine Power as female in nature. That this message is coming freely from a man conveys, for me, an extra level of healing in this regard. In addition, because Kaleshwar states that Mary was "ninety-nine percent equal to Mother Divine,"[4] he is affirming what I noted in chapter 3, that she was nothing less than an avatar—a living incarnation—of the Great Goddess.

Kaleshwar says something else about Mary's elevated status that is very important, and that I only hinted about in the previous chapter: Mary did not end up being as powerful as she was through some kind of automatic grace. She earned it. And Kaleshwar tells us a bit about how she did that. He states that Mary received the full blessings of Mother Divine and achieved unification with Her by meditating for many, many lifetimes "on the Creation."[5] In other words, she had incarnated as a soul many times, always studying and absorbing the reality of the Divine until she was able to fully merge with it. As a result, Kaleshwar affirms, her being came into its most recent incarnation, the one we know as "Mother Mary," as a "divine soul." Although Kaleshwar does not talk about Mary's birth from her mother Anne, his observations indeed correspond with my own regarding Mary's avatar nature by virtue of her being a "divinely conceived" soul.

What's more, Kaleshwar tells us, Mary engaged in profound yogic practices "under the direct guidance of the Mother" in order to "create Jesus's soul."[6] With this Kaleshwar is directly asserting what has been thickly veiled even in Mary's infancy gospel. I have attempted to shed light on some of these "yogic practices" by looking at the hidden meanings behind the words and symbols regarding her training and divine birth ritual in my previous book, *The Mystery Tradition of Miraculous Conception*. But Kaleshwar's revelations explain much more about this—and they firmly locate Mary's power in her bodily womb.

This brings us to the critical but much-overlooked aspect of the Holy Womb Chakra as being an essential aspect of the Divine Feminine. Kaleshwar teaches us that the energy he calls "Mother Divine" is the supreme Creator, though she does not create through what I call the "erector set" model of creation that has been handed down to us through the Hebrew Bible. Rather she has created through her own womb chakra, or energy center. She is the Great Mother, capable of birthing all things through her universal womb—which is really all of Creation itself.

THE HOLY WOMB CHAKRA—
OF MARY AND ALL WOMEN

The critical matter here is that, according to Kaleshwar, by virtue of being a replica of Mother Divine, Mother Mary also possessed the holiest of Holy Womb Chakras. I'll pause here to note that the idea that Mother Mary possessed the entire power of creation within herself is not news to the Christian tradition. Early Christian poets also saw her as enclosing the entirety of heaven and earth in her very womb—depicted within the image of a single round rose.[7] So in this sense Kaleshwar's views are in fact in alignment with what has gone before us in the West.

Remarkably Kaleshwar asserts that *all* women can access this original, creative womb energy of the Mother. Physically I identify the womb chakra as extending from the navel to the vulva and including all aspects of the uterus in between. Women's womb chakras make women walking representatives of Mother Divine. But most of us do not realize that . . . yet. I believe that these revelations about Mary will allow many more of us to awaken to this reality and to understand how we may use it to heal and elevate our world.

Kaleshwar says that the womb chakra of the woman is extremely powerful, far more so than we have ever realized. He elaborates:

> Through your womb chakra you can do miracles. You can manifest a physical body. You can change one thing to another thing. You can change a person's mind. You can do a distance healing from where you are to any person, anywhere on the planet. . . . The channels are there. It all depends on how pure your womb chakra energy is.[8]

He adds that if loved properly by a man, a woman's womb chakra can help a king literally win an empire, but if it has caused harm or heartbreak it can create a "kind of little tsunami" and can lead to a man's downfall. "The woman's womb chakra has that much capacity," Kaleshwar says.[9]

In fact he outright declares that because women possess the womb chakra in their bodies, they are far more powerful than men on energetic and spiritual levels, and are able to advance spiritually at a much faster pace. "The womb is the direct channel and the most direct highway to receive the energy," he says.[10] It is for this reason that most holy men have relied on women for "receiving light," and why "99.999 percent of the saints received the spiritual powers from the Mother's [Mother Divine's] womb."[11]

Kaleshwar makes it clear, however, that although only a woman has a womb chakra on the *physical* level, a man possesses a womb chakra at the *soul* level. Moreover, a man can access the physical womb chakra by connecting spiritually to his mother's womb, even if she is no longer alive.[12]

He can also do so by connecting emotionally and/or sexually to a woman with whom he shares mutual unconditional love—that is, a soul mate.

According to Kaleshwar Mother Mary was deeply aware of her womb chakra as a portal for creating life and conducting all kinds of healings, and it is through this capacity that she can, even now, serve as a teacher, especially to women. He reports that the ancient palm leaf manuscripts reveal that Mary was involved in a host of specific "yogic practices" not only to bring Jesus into her womb but also to teach Jesus while he was gestating, as well as during his life. Even more fascinating, Kaleshwar says that these practices allowed the Blessed Mother to use her Holy Womb Chakra to help resurrect her murdered son *in full bodily form*, which I will discuss shortly.

The "yogic practices" Kaleshwar refers to have nothing to do with the physical postures that the West has come to understand as yoga. He describes them, rather, as sacred activities that involve all of the following: regularly communicating with Mother Divine and her messenger angels through meditation; cultivating an unconditionally loving heart; working with sacred objects that have been imbued with power by other masters in specific ways; communing with and absorbing the energy of particular power spots on the planet; and working in tandem with a soul mate.

Significantly Mary's yogas also included opening certain channels and energy centers of the body by chanting sacred mantras, and by drawing and contemplating complex sacred symbols known as yantras—all of which were recorded on the ancient "palm leaf manuscripts" mentioned earlier. The use of these sounds and symbols can eventually confer powers on the advanced practitioner—such as the ability to heal others seemingly miraculously, to bring dead bodies to life, to command matter, water, fire, and air to do one's bidding, and more.

MARY'S CREATION OF JESUS

Kaleshwar tells us that Mary perfected and implemented all of these yogas. He reports that she had the greatest ability a human can possess for "talking with the angels"—that is, those advisers on the inner planes of reality—and that she sat in meditation with them in the early hours each morning. "She talked about the universe, about the Creation, about soul mechanisms," he says of their conversation.[13] He also tells us that Mary was able to communicate with Mother Divine directly, and that she obtained many of her spiritual powers in this way.

The decision to bring Jesus into the world, Kaleshwar states, came through a conversation Mary had on one occasion with Mother Divine in which she asked for a way to "control the negativity on the planet." Mother Divine's response was that because Mary herself, being female, was an integral part of nature and creation, she could not become this kind of aggressive "commander" in the age into which she had incarnated. While in an earlier epoch the fierce "demon-destroyer" goddess Kali had been able to take on such a role without harm to herself, Mary's taking on such a role in her time would have caused her to receive "unbelievable negativity in her heart."*[14] Such a role could only properly be fulfilled by a male she could bring forth from her body— a son who would possess the energy of the Sacred Masculine in the form the Hindus call Shiva. Mary agreed to bring such a son to the planet, and this was granted to her through the blessing of Mother Divine.

Kaleshwar also says something striking in this regard: "All Jesus's energy was nothing but his mother's energy."[15] I believe this statement affirms for us the idea I mentioned in chapter 3 and discuss more extensively in my book *The Mystery Tradition of Miraculous Conception*, that Mary's divine conception was brought about not by connection with a male god or priest–king, but rather through parthenogenesis. This means she had nothing to do with "the Father" impregnating her—the

---

*However, Kaleshwar notes (in *Real Life*, 63) that now women may once again indeed address planetary negativity themselves in a way Mary could not by calling on male (Shiva) power through invoking the energy of male teachers associated with Kaleshwar's lineage.

story we have been handed down in Christianity. According to what Kaleshwar is saying, Jesus was, indeed, "all Mary." He was her sovereign, parthenogenetic co-creation with Mother Divine.

Kaleshwar also points out that Jesus's birth on the planet was his very first incarnation as a soul. The fact that he was "a pure crystal soul that came from Mother Divine," not one who had already incarnated in other lifetimes, was a particular mark of his greatness.[16] In this, Jesus was something of a "bookend" companion to his mother, who, as mentioned, had had the opposite experience of perfecting herself through many, many lifetimes.

Although Kaleshwar does not comment directly on the mechanisms of Mary's divine conception of Jesus, he does briefly explain how Mother Divine (in some traditions known as Parvati) divinely created her son, the Hindu god Ganesh:

Mother Divine manifested *Lord Ganesh* out of sandalwood powder using Her womb chakra. She created a baby by sending Her womb the chakra energy—this is a very important point—to give life to that sandalwood powder. That powder turned into a baby. That is Ganesh.[17]

In other words Kaleshwar is implying that by using some kind of "seeding material" and sending "chakra energy" (that is, universal life force power) to her Holy Womb Chakra, any avatar of Mother Divine— which Mary was—can conceive without the help of male energy.

The closest we get in the Christian writings to what Kaleshwar is saying can be found in the Infancy Gospel of James/Birth of Mary. There the Blessed Mother's conception of Jesus is said to have happened through her drawing on the power of the universal life force energy— identified there as the *logos*. As I discuss in *The Mystery Tradition of Miraculous Conception*, this logos is essentially feminine—the wisdom energy of Sophia as Universal Mother. The specific process Mary engaged in as she sent this power to her womb is described in the gospel as "spinning" and "weaving," which I contend is the Christian way of naming the "yoga" she was enacting.*

It is quite interesting, then, that Kaleshwar shared through his teachings about the Holy Womb Chakra that Mary used the mantras from the palm leaf manuscripts (which are mainly in Sanskrit) in order to 1) open up her power channels for bringing Jesus into being, and 2) teach him much of what he needed to know,† for Sanskrit mantras essentially are composed of words that can be broken down into "seed syllables," or what are known as bijaksharas (or bijas, for short). These are considered to be none other than the seed sounds of the universe, and each seed sound, according to Kaleshwar, is a powerful vibration of a particular angelic being.††

While the idea that Mary chanted mantras resonant with the tones of the angels may sound far-fetched to the average Christian, remarkably we do find a suggestion of this in Infancy Gospel of James/Birth of Mary. There we learn that while Mary was being trained in the temple in her role as a divine birth priestess, she "heard the hymns" of "holy messengers," that is, angels. And the logos that she connected with was

---

*For my discussion of logos as Sophia, see Rigoglioso, *Mystery Tradition*, 103–105. For more on my discussion of Mary's process of spinning and weaving in the conception of Jesus, see 101–2.

†As Sri Kaleshwar's senior student Monika of Penukona (Mataji) states, "According to the palm leaf manuscripts, these were the same meditations and practices that Mary did when Jesus was in her Womb" (Mataji et al., *The Holy Womb*, 3). Mary's use of these mantras, which Kaleshwar also refers to throughout his works and teachings as "channels," is implied in his discussion of her prayer and meditation practice, 61–62 of *Real Life*. See also Mataji et al., *The Holy Womb*, 147, where Kaleshwar states, "Mother Mary [. . .] sent Jesus's soul again back into his body through chanting certain perfect bijaksharas [syllables that compose the mantras]." See also "What Is in the Palm Leaf Manuscripts" section of the Monika of Penukonda website, where Monika writes, "The palm leaf manuscripts [. . .] contain the body of knowledge that Jesus, Mary, and Mary Magdalen practiced. They contain a body of ancient spiritual wisdom, a soul science, that gives tools to develop the divine spark in the soul." This body of knowledge most definitely included specific mantras, which are shared by various teachers who have been trained in the lineage of Sri Kaleshwar.

††See Mataji et al., *The Holy Womb*, 20–21, and also 304, where Kaleshwar refers to the bijas as "blooming stars."

understood to be the *divine word* or, perhaps more accurately, the *divine sound*. I identify this divine sound as the primary sound of the universe, or the great OM.[18] The OM is certainly a regular feature of Sanskrit mantras, as any mala-sporting practitioner knows well!

So it's clear even from the apocryphal Christian tradition that Mary was working with sound frequencies as part of her divine birth practices. Kaleshwar is adding to our knowledge that the sound frequencies took the form of mantras—that is, *sounds connected with the angelic realms*. Putting all of this together, we can read in Kaleshwar's teachings that part of Mary's drawing on the sacred sound power of Universal Mother/Sophia *specifically involved her chanting these mantras intently while sending energy to her womb for the purposes of divine conception*. It was angelic chants in particular, then, that served as the "seeding material" for Jesus and which accompanied the "spinning" and "weaving" process Mary engaged in to conceive him parthenogenetically.

One thing I find enormously healing about Kaleshwar's revelations is that he restores the Great Mother to her rightful place as the universal creator and orchestrator of the dramatic events that took place around Mary and Jesus. I have always felt disturbed by the New Testament statements attributed to Jesus in which it is translated that he credits his "father in heaven" with his origin and the source of his power. Kaleshwar verifies my own understanding that the advent of Jesus was basically a willed project on the part of a Great Feminine Energy who felt the need to bring healing to a part of her creation that had run amok. His work provides us with further details that enable us to fully grasp the power of Mother Divine and Mary's cooperation with her in that great healing. At last! As Kaleshwar himself says, "Two thousand years later the information is finally coming out."[19]

MARY'S SACRED PRACTICES

One of Kaleshwar's most remarkable contributions to our understanding of Mary is his description of her early morning practice. He tells us that through this practice she not only perfected herself spiritually, but she brought enlightenment to Jesus while he was in the womb; she conveyed upon him his full status as an avatar of Mother Divine. This puts the full ascension of Jesus in Mary's hands, something we will see amplified when we look at her role at the time of his crucifixion—a powerful role indeed!

Kaleshwar's description helps us fill in some of the gaps in the Infancy Gospel of James/Birth of Mary, helping us understand yet more about what the young Mary learned from her mother Anne and the temple virgins who raised her to be a priestess of divine birth and a fully ascended master. At the same time, it brings her down to earth, personalizing her for us as a living and breathing woman who had a specific routine, and who had to keep up with it like anyone else in order to reap its benefits.

According to Kaleshwar, like most saints, Mary slept and dreamt from 11 p.m. to 2 a.m., woke up and meditated from 2 to 3 a.m., and then communicated with the angels from 3 to 5 a.m. While conversing with the angels herself, he says, she was also connecting Jesus to the angels and was directly teaching him through them.[20] As we just learned, "communicating with the angels" probably means that Mary chanted her mantras during these two hours.

Remarkably this echoes some of what we find in an apocryphal thirteenth-century tract by Jacobus da Voragine, *The Golden Legend*. The following statement is attributed in that text to a letter written by St. Jerome:

[T]he Blessed Virgin had made a rule for herself: the time from dawn to the third hour she devoted to prayer, from the third to the ninth hour she worked at weaving, and from the ninth hour on she prayed without stopping until an angel appeared and brought her food.[21]

Interestingly in this Christian-based text again we see the reference to Mary "weaving." I would suggest that this activity that Mary was engaged in for six hours in the early morning was of another order entirely—a continuing yogic womb practice that allowed her not only to conceive Jesus, but also to send telepathic teachings to him prior to his birth. I would also contend that this "weaving" was something she continued throughout her life as a means of keeping her womb powers strong for their expression in the form of the healings and other miracles she performed, which we'll hear about in chapter 5. As we have learned from Kaleshwar, all of these powers are indeed possible through a highly purified and amplified Holy Womb Chakra. And St. Jerome here is verifying that these kinds of practices allowed Mary to purify and greatly empower herself on every level.

Kaleshwar further says that as a result of these spiritual practices, in the first month of her pregnancy, Mary fully sealed her unification with Mother Divine. In the second month, she learned how to control the five elements (earth, air, fire, water, and ether).[22] Through this she received what are called the *siddhis*, that is, various supernatural powers that seem to defy the laws of the material plane. Classically, examples of siddhis include the ability to do things like fly through the air, walk through solid obstructions, dive into the ground, tread on water, and so forth.* This means that Mary was a master who could most likely "walk on water" well before Jesus, and that she was the one who conveyed these miracle abilities to her son. Again, we see in Kaleshwar's teachings an elevation of this great female master to a level that we've never imagined before.

Kaleshwar tells us that in the third month of her pregnancy, Mary acquired another very important ability: she learned how to enter a body and make it come alive after it had just died. This is known as the yoga that the Hindu Vedas call *parakaya pravesh*. The Hindu saint notes that this latter accomplishment firmly established her as a master on the planet.[23] He tell us that she used this skill to assist Jesus during and after the crucifixion, as we will learn more about later. Again, to discover that

---

*For more on siddhis, see, for example, McAfee. The siddhi entry in good old Wikipedia also offers an excellent discussion of the topic, with further references.

Jesus was not the only one who knew how to bring the dead to life, and that Mary was the master of this art before him, is quite stunning. It raises the power profile of the Blessed Mother enormously.

Kaleshwar's extraordinary revelations don't end there. He tells us that *every* mother is capable of bringing enlightenment to her gestating child by engaging in similar processes! In his Holy Womb Chakra teachings, he provides a means by which a couple can begin this process by first conceiving what he calls a "divine child." This involves chanting two mantras, one of which is done by both partners during sexual union and the other of which is chanted by the mother as much as possible once the conception has occurred. The process also includes other mantras that a mother can use during pregnancy, birthing, and on into the life of the child to help that child receive advancements and protections. The implication is that these mantras were all part of Mary's private practice. Such Marian technologies therefore can serve as a resource for all women to cultivate elevated children—and this is one of the key pieces of the Holy Womb Chakra teachings. Yes, clearing, healing, and empowering the womb by using the same mantras that Mary used is a pathway open to all of us, one that has now been made available through teachers trained in Kaleshwar's lineage.*

MARY'S SOUL-MATED RELATIONSHIP WITH JESUS

As we have seen, Kaleshwar maintains that before and after Jesus's birth, Mary was *his* teacher, and not the other way around. She was the master from whom her son learned much of what he needed for his own ministry. This is another point on which Kaleshwar corrects the traditional image that Christianity portrays of the relationship between Mary and Jesus—something that for me was immediately and deeply healing when I learned of it.

---

*The on-demand course The Holy Womb Chakra Teachings, available online at Seven Sisters Mystery School, offers such instruction.

This idea is not unheard of in the Christian writings themselves, which I was surprised to discover with a little exploration into the apocrypha. We find a hint of it in the Christian writing known as *The Life of the Virgin*, the earliest complete biography of Mary. The author of this text is thought to be Maximus the Confessor (580–662), an important theologian of the early Byzantine period. He was probably working from very early manuscripts, among them the Infancy Gospel of James/Birth of Mary as well as others that are likely lost to us. What's important to what we'll learn from this biography is that Maximus may be reflecting lost traditions that once circulated in late antiquity.[24] That is, his words may be revealing details about Mary's life that were recorded by early scribes who had access to her authentic history.

It is thus fascinating, then, that in *The Life of the Virgin* we learn that, as a child, Jesus did not "make use of any human assistance except from his holy and all-blessed mother."[25] While the implication here is that Jesus came to earth possessing much of the spiritual knowledge he needed, there is something in this statement that we see nowhere else in the Christian cannon. It is clearly telling us that Jesus indeed relied on his mother not only for his birth, but also for his learning. In this, I believe that the author is touching upon a similar stream of information as Kaleshwar.

The real mind-opener for me was Kaleshwar's assertion that Mother Mary was Jesus's best friend—nothing less than his "soul mate."[26] To be clear, this relationship was not sexual (in contrast to the one between Jesus and Mary Magdalene, which I will discuss in chapter 5). Rather, it was a spiritual soul mating. This means that Mother Mary was the one who knew everything about her son, was the one he confided in, and was the one to whom he would pray first for blessings and power when he started healing anyone.

According to Kaleshwar the two shared true unconditional love, and it was this energy that Jesus drew on in order to heal others and restore the dead to life. Without this power, the Hindu saint says—which is essentially the power of Mary's Holy Womb Chakra—Jesus would not have been able to perform his dramatic healings and miracles.[27] All of this adds another layer of understanding to the statement we find in the Gospel of Philip (59) that the Blessed Mother "always traveled with Jesus." She was his constant, abiding friend, advisor, and confidante.

This again finds validation in Maximus's *The Life of the Virgin*, where Mary's natural bond with Jesus, and her supreme understanding of him on every level, are beautifully depicted. In this narrative we are told that she was "bound to him in soul and body," and that she was totally like him in valor and virtue.[28] Echoing *Philip*'s glimpse of Mary always walking or traveling with Jesus, Maximus writes, "the all-holy Virgin and mother of the Lord remained inseparable" from her son. "Wherever he went, she went with him, and she was considered the life and the light of his eyes and soul, going with him and listening to his words."[29] *Mary as the life and light of Jesus's eyes and soul.* This affirms what Kaleshwar is telling us, and illuminates an immense power within Mary that we haven't heard much about.

Maximus also emphasizes the soul bond between the two in his description of the events spanning from the time of Jesus's interrogation by Pilate to the period after the crucifixion. Mary remained near Jesus, seeing everything and hearing his words. "Mentally she was joined to her sweet son and what was happening to him," Maximus tells us. Not only was Mother Mary "inseparable" from Jesus, but she also "shared his pain."[30]

In a world in which the mother-son relationship has become a Freudian minefield, the moving glimpse that Kaleshwar gives us of an authentic, exalted, supportive, and pure love between a mother and her son is a healing balm in and of itself. The fact that it is verified in the Christian apocrypha validates Kaleshwar's important revelations and lends credence to everything else he says about Mary and Jesus that we are exploring, as well.

MARY'S RESURRECTION OF JESUS THROUGH HER WOMB CHAKRA

As we have seen, it was Mary who helped Jesus anchor his powers while he was in her womb. The Christian tradition confirms that he further developed supernatural powers—the ability to change water into wine, walk on water, heal people, resurrect the dead, come back to life after his own death, and more. In short, he acquired the siddhis. Kaleshwar says Jesus perfected these powers in India by studying with masters and using the practices offered on the palm leaf manuscripts.*

As mentioned earlier, according to Kaleshwar, the Blessed Mother herself learned how to bring the dead back to life, a yogic power known as parakaya pravesh.† The Hindu saint affirms that Jesus also acquired this power, and the idea that he accomplished it through the dedicated use of special mantras and other practices demystifies how he could raise Lazarus out of the tomb, which we hear about in John 11:38–43. Kaleshwar tells us that Jesus also perfected *atma khandana* yoga, which is the process of bringing one's soul out of one's body, dividing it into parts, and then receiving it back into one's body.[31] These abilities turned out to be critical when it came time for the crucifixion.

As Kaleshwar explains, when Jesus's broken body was taken from the cross and put into the cave that served as his tomb, Mother Mary took him on her lap, as Michelangelo portrays it in his dramatic sculpture *La Pietá*. Kaleshwar describes what she did to resurrect Jesus, body and soul, with these remarkable and moving words:

> She took Jesus's dead body in her lap, then connected Mother Divine's womb chakra to her womb. Mary started to use one channel [a mantra from the palm leaf manuscript] to make Jesus's consciousness aware. Jesus had already learned it, knew it, and practiced it. She used the womb chakra to heal everything that had happened to Jesus at the crucifixion—getting physically wounded, mentally tortured, heartfully crying and disturbed on the soul level. She gave initiation to Jesus, chanting Shiva bijaksharas [sacred syllables specifically connected with the powers of the god Shiva]. These prayers

---

*See Kaleshwar, *Real Life*, 85–119, for a discussion of Jesus's trainings in India.
†*Para* means "another," and *kaya* means "structure." Kaleshwar, *Real Life*, 105.

are like power numbers, like using your cell number, to call the soul. Mary regenerated Jesus through her womb chakra, then she sent Jesus's soul back to his body to make him alive.

Then it started. It was like huge lightning wave to the body. Finally Khandana Yoga happened. Jesus then started to regenerate what was completely broken. What your western mind calls the crucifixion is called Khandana Yoga in the Indian system. Regenerating what was completely broken. . . .

It was only possible through Mary's womb chakra energy. It is written on the palm leaves that every creation, every miracle, only happens through womb chakra energy. Without that, it's impossible.[32]

When Cindy Lindsay shared this quote in the Holy Womb Chakra course, a hush fell over those of us in the class. The idea that Mary's Holy Womb Chakra could "birth" her son a second time sent enormous power throughout my being. I felt as though my consciousness had passed through a portal into a new dimension.

Cindy also told us of another means by which Mary helped bring Jesus back to life: washing his body with a powerful ash from burned wood. Such ash, when used in such a way by a master who has gained a "command" over it, is known as *vibhuti*.[33]

All of this was completely profound and new to me, yet it wasn't new. First of all this information validated a teaching I had received in a sacred medicine ceremony years earlier, whereby I was shown that a woman could process the souls of the unrestful dead back through her womb and into the light. In the ceremony I was even called upon to practice this on a stream of my own ancestors. I therefore knew from that experience that the womb was a portal of both life and death. But hearing about Mary's work with Jesus in this regard was taking the power of the womb to a whole new level.

Second, the motif of a "huge lightning wave" being involved in Jesus's resurrection seemed like the mirror image of the "flash of light" that was involved in the parthenogenetic conception of a child. I discussed this briefly in chapter 3 and more extensively in *The Mystery Tradition of Miraculous Conception*,[34] and such imagery is depicted in various paintings about Mary's conception of Jesus. Having this validation of what I had also received in the parallel context felt like a further verification of Kaleshwar's information.

Holy, holy, holy.

Do we find any corroborating evidence of Mary being at the tomb in any of the apocryphal gospels? In fact we do. Again, in Maximus's *The Life of the Virgin*, we hear the extraordinary account that Mary secures Jesus's body from Pontius Pilate and inters him in the tomb when the apostles flee in fear. She is able to do this with the help of Joseph of Arimathea and a disciple known as Nicodemus, but even they depart, leaving her to keep a constant vigil at the tomb—where we are told she witnesses the resurrection.[35] This account, which is ignored in the New Testament, gives us valid time windows in which precisely what Kaleshwar reports indeed could have taken place—Mary holding her son's body for a time in private so as to continue the mantras and engage the parakaya pravesh resurrection yoga using her womb powers.

Another fascinating and powerful yoga that Jesus masterfully carried forth was the ability to command the "kala chakra," that is, the phenomenon of time. Kaleshwar tells us that at the climactic moments of his crucifixion, as his soul was preparing to exit his body, Jesus went back in time, to ten days before the crucifixion:

[U]sing the Atma Khandana process, Jesus took the majority of his soul out and merged in the Divinity. He left a small piece in his body. . . . The reason for leaving a part of the soul in the body is, if the soul gets injured and the body very damaged, one soul part can fix the other parts. The soul part can heal and re-manifest the entire physical body.[36]

According to Kaleshwar this process involved Jesus "stopping his breath" nine minutes before he knew he was to leave his body[37]—a siddhic ability that demonstrated his great mastery over the "air" element.

Kaleshwar says that through these yogas Mary and Jesus were able to restore his body to life—that is, to resurrect him. At some point after these dramatic events, Jesus was accompanied to India with the assistance of unnamed holy people from that region of the world. Many of his students eventually traveled to join him. He spent twelve years in the Himalayas in the northeast belt of India, where Kaleshwar says there is evidence of his presence in sculpture and rock inscriptions in the Badrinath and Kedernath mountains. Then Jesus traveled and stayed in southern India, in Penukonda in particular. Mary Magdalene, his wife, joined him there, had children with him, and helped him write certain palm leaf manuscripts. According to Kaleshwar, their bloodline still exists throughout the globe.[38]

This timeline about Jesus's fate on the cross is different from those others may hold, including some who have received direct revelation. The idea that Jesus never actually died during the crucifixion is not entirely new, however. We see this claim in one contested section of the Islamic Qur'an (4:157–59), for example. Interestingly, as I see it, the ambiguous text here leaves some wiggle room for Kaleshwar's interpretation of the events—which could even be used to reconcile the longstanding discord between Muslims and Christians on this matter.* Certain gnostic sources similarly deny the crucifixion, and even some of the canonical gospels could be read as indicating that after the crucifixion Jesus reappeared fully walking around in his flesh suit.†

Could it be that Jesus's soul never fully left the earth plane, or that he was resurrected not just into the interdimensional realms but back into his body? Could he indeed have traveled back to India, where he had also spent some of his younger years, as Kaleshwar claims? Again

---

*For a discussion on this section of the *Qur'an*, see, for example, Wayne, "The Quran, the Crucifixion, and the Gnostics."

†For Jesus's meeting with the disciples after the crucifixion, see John 20:26–27 and Luke 24:39. For related gnostic references, see, for example, Wayne, "The Quran, the Crucifixion, and the Gnostics."

what I would suggest is that rather than getting into arguments about what is "real" or "true," we consider holding *all* possible historical timelines as containing something authentic. The point is, each possibility will appeal to different people based on the soul lessons they need to learn. By holding difference in this way, we are also moving closer to embodying the teachings of unconditional love that Mary and Jesus taught.

Kaleshwar claims that even before his birth, "Jesus Christ made a commitment with the Mother. . . . He made a deal with Her to bring the supernatural information to the planet."[39] Jesus's aim, he says, was to have others become powerful healers and masters like himself by engaging the mantras and studying the yantras, the sacred diagrams, he used. The same is true of Mother Mary, who used many of the same chants and drawings to fully embody divine power. A third of the manuscripts containing this information, says Kaleshwar, remains in India, another third can be found in Europe, and a full third has been destroyed.[40]

According to Kaleshwar, the "channels" to clear and elevate one's own womb capacities—the mantras, yantras, and associated practices that he has pulled from the sands of time—can be accessed by *anyone* who wants to put in the time and focus to reap their benefits.* This will allow us collectively not only to put together a picture about the past that serves our growth, but also to figure out how we are going to use the information going forward to elevate humanity. This is the work of being a "Mary," an idea I will discuss more fully in the epilogue.

A CAUTION ABOUT THIS INFORMATION

There is one thing I have not told you. One of the apocryphal writings known as the Gospel of Bartholomew also provides stunning mystical

---

*Again, these practices can be accessed through the Holy Womb Chakra Teachings online at Seven Sisters Mystery School.

information about the nature of Mary's conception of Jesus. This gospel could have been written as early as the second century,[41] and I contend that its great antiquity supports the idea that it a reliable source of authentic information. I wish to discuss what this gospel depicts as both a revelation and a caution.

In this intriguing text Mary is approached by some of the male apostles who express rapt curiosity about "how she conceived the incomprehensible, or how she bare him that cannot be carried, or how she brought forth so much greatness."[42] In short, they are asking her point blank how she accomplished the feat of divine conception. At first Mary hesitates about revealing this information, making the startling comment, "If I should begin to tell you, fire will issue forth out of my mouth and consume all the world." Clearly that is some potent information! When the apostles persist, she decides to speak about it, but she first establishes some very interesting conditions indicating that she must create a sacred container in order for the information to be revealed.

Mary's curious instructions begin after she is given the honor of leading a prayer, which for her consists of an impassioned praise of the Divine. At that point, she sits down and tells two apostles to come close to her on either side, and for each one to hold her under an armpit. She sets another one in front of her to hold her chest, and yet another one behind her to touch his knees up against her back and hold her shoulders. This, she says, is to protect herself, "lest when I begin to speak my bones be loosed one from another." Clearly, she is preparing them for something energetically huge that will have ripples throughout her human body.

Mary then begins her extraordinary explanation of how she conceived Jesus. She tells the apostles present that one day while she was being raised in the temple and receiving her food from a divine messenger (a motif that is echoed in the Infancy Gospel of James/Birth of Mary), a great being appeared to her whose face was "incomprehensible." Upon seeing this being, Mary had the sense of the earth trembling. She was then thrown to the ground, completely unable to look at him for very long. This messenger lifted her up, baptized her with water, gave her bread and wine, and told her that she was the chosen vessel to conceive a son who would be of great service to the world.*

The Gospel of Bartholomew (2:22) tells us that after explaining these events, then and there, in front of the apostles, the extraordinary thing that Mary had been preparing them for by having them hold her body indeed took place. The narrative tells us:

> And as she was saying this, fire issued out of her mouth; and the world was at the point to come to an end: but Jesus appeared quickly and laid his hand upon her mouth and said unto Mary: Utter not this mystery, or this day my whole creation will come to an end (and the flame from her mouth ceased). And the apostles were taken with fear lest haply the Lord should be wroth with them.

I was utterly struck with the enormity of this account. It tells us that the very details of Mary's conception of Jesus apparently carried such a power that they could literally be earth shattering if verbalized. Apparently, in revealing them out loud, Mary came perilously close to jeopardizing the entire existence of the earth plane.

Perhaps the tsunami-like force of this information is partly why the concept and details about divine birth as a living reality have been suppressed to this day. They hold the power to "destroy" the Earth—and I would argue that to some degree they have already been used in this way. As I discuss in *The Mystery Tradition of Miraculous Conception*, divine birth was ultimately co-opted to bring to the earth plane the heroes who led the destruction of women's institutions of power and the

---

*Of interest here is the fact that Mary describes the encounter as taking place directly in the temple. This contrasts with the version of the Infancy Gospel of James/Birth of Mary that is most popularly consulted, which denotes the angelic encounters as taking place at Joseph's home and the local well after Mary has been ejected from the temple owing to her menarche. By indicating that the conception took place in the temple, Bartholomew is thus affirming Mary's continued residency there beyond her girlhood, an important point that emphasizes her role as a priestess. See, Rigoglioso, *Mystery Tradition*, 87.

spread of patriarchy on the planet. This was the case with the children of numerous divine birth priestesses of the last two thousand years, such as Theseus, Perseus, Heracles, and Alexander the (so-called) Great.

I believe that the practice of divine birth continued to be hijacked over the centuries so as to birth lineages, including royal lines, that became increasingly destructive to the well-being of humanity. This is the case with the divine birth processes that seems to have plagued historical figures such as Queen Guinevere, King Arthur, and the mage Merlin, not to mention latter-day royal personages and the progeny of various high-status power bloodlines.*

On the other hand we can also look upon this power of divine birth as a living reality in its positive valence—meaning that a proper understanding of its mysteries can "utterly transform" the earth, rather than destroy it. In order for divine conception to be understood and used properly, though, people must be spiritually ready to comprehend what it is truly about. Otherwise it is likely to be continually co-opted, misused, and turned destructive.

Have we come to the point where people are ready to hold this knowledge? Are there women on the planet who can engage in divine conception with integrity, and for the right reasons? I believe we are indeed ready for this information, and that in fact we need it now. We've come to the place where continuing to keep it under wraps has become more problematic than bringing it to the light.

Clearly, however, in our realm of duality divine birth is a double-edged sword. Powerful information like this can provoke a wave of resistance on the part of forces who don't want to see the ban on women's womb empowerment lifted. As I mentioned in chapter 3, Jesus and John the Baptist were in danger of being killed as soon as authorities got wind of their divine births, which sent their mothers

---

*More information about this can be found in the courses Healing the Womb 3, and Heal Yourself and Our World by Reclaiming Guinevere, Arthur, the Fae & the Round Table, accessible online at Seven Sisters Mystery School.

on the run. In contemporary times I know three women who claim to have conceived children through sacred non-ordinary means—and two of the children did, in fact, die early.* There is only one child I am aware of whose mother claims to have conceived her through divine parthenogenesis who has grown to adulthood and seems to be out of harm's way. Is this because her mother lives each day as a very advanced spiritual adept in India and has the protective forces needed to help her child survive?

What else is needed for the world—and for people's personal lives—not to split apart when divine birth becomes a living, spoken reality?

Maureen Walton, a spiritual teacher and fine artist who has studied and painted various public murals of the divine birth story of the great Haudenosaunee (Iroquois) leader known as the Peacemaker, believes that the cultivation of a mother-daughter-child lineage is critical in order for a divine child to be protected. In that history, the young mother Gehedosug had the training and support of her mother, Gaheliogaha.† Maureen and I have discussed how Mary had the same kind of support from her mother, Anne. I would add that, as we have seen in the case of Mary, who was part of a community of temple virgins, the divinely conceiving woman must be surrounded by a group of similarly trained and supportive priestesses. Perhaps only this kind of lineage and group training and protection can provide her with all of what she needs so as to bring to term a healthy holy child, and so as to make sure that the child lives to fulfill its divine mission.

In order for women to be ready not only to conceive but also to sustain a divine child, they must be working on their own spiritual advancement, as well, purifying their hearts, wombs, and souls. When

---

*See, for example, Den Poitras's story of "Laurie's" child in *Parthenogenesis*, 95–113. There is also the case of a child of another woman I know personally, whose name I will not mention here to protect her.

†Maureen Walton has expressed this view in various conversations with me and teachings since 2015; see also Walton O'Brien, *The Good Darkness*, 286–96, for her recounting of the story of Gehedosug and Gaheliogaha.

I have taught about divine birth in the past, I have had a number of women communicate to me that they wish to produce a divinely conceived child. I can see that such a wish is frequently coming more from place of ego than a place of love and spiritual service, and that the quality of integrity needed to be working at such a soul level is still a work in progress on the planet. Given the possible misuse of the practice that has taken place, the degree of impeccability on the part of a holy woman required for a truly world-serving divine birth cannot be over emphasized, and, I contend, is a rarity on the earth plane today. Perhaps my books on Mary will inspire discussion about what women really need to develop within themselves to conceive true avatars who will walk among us.

There is the deeper question, too, as to whether divine birth is perhaps even an outdated technology. Over the past two thousand years and more, the message of the Marys and Jesus is being felt more strongly across the planet: we can advance to full divinity *within ourselves* and become the living avatars our world needs. Maybe we are looking at a case of both/and. Perhaps in this great drama of human healing and evolution there is a role for divine birth priestesses to bring in avatars who can help those of us who would like to cultivate our own spirituality and achieve the *personal* ascension/IN-scension that is being much talked about.

Whatever the case may be, and whatever level of womb advancement a woman wishes to achieve, through the journey of this chapter we are now more aware of the fact that many expanded womb powers are available to all of us—whatever our sex. By seeing Mary as a practitioner, a woman who accomplished the earth walk many times and assiduously used her tools daily to cultivate her inner womb temple, we can see her more clearly as a mentor for our own spiritual growth, rather than a deity to be worshipped. And by understanding that her tools are readily available to us, we know we have at least one method of walking the path along with her.

CHAPTER 4 INTEGRATION ACTIVITY

Mary's Womb Powers

I invite you to write down your impressions of the following in your Mary Journal.

- How did the idea that Mother Mary may have resurrected Jesus through her own womb land for you? What are your thoughts and feelings about this?

- What else is getting stirred within as you consider Mary's womb practices and powers—and the possibility that these practices are available to you?

.... Online Guided Meditation ....

Receiving Comfort and Clarity through Mother Mary's Holy Womb

In this journey, you will release your woes to Mother Mary and receive divine comfort in return. Her potent light will encode and heal your DNA, reconstructing strands that have become frayed in the tension of challenging times, and providing fortification for any difficulties that may arise in the future. See page 150 to register for the free meditations.

CHAPTER 5

Mary as Healer, Mentor, and Women's Champion

We now have a much fuller picture of Mary up until the time she gave birth to Jesus. But who did Mary the priestess, this powerful master of womb mysteries, become after that? What did her ministry consist of as she grew into adulthood during the life of Jesus and after his death? And how is this relevant to our lives today?

There is so little said about Mary's life in the New Testament and even in her infancy gospel that we must turn elsewhere to find out more. As we have begun to see in exploring Maximus's *The Life of the Virgin*, there *are* other documents containing information about Mary—texts that were widely held to be sacred around the Mediterranean world in the early centuries after Christ, in which we learn that she became a significant religious leader and a master healer.[1]

These depictions of Mary are hardly a matter of fantasy; they do in fact correspond with authentic, well-documented roles of women in early Christianity. What pleasantly surprised me was the discovery that women were in the majority in heading up the early churches—or, at the very least, they were more publicly visible than the men. The historical writings show women preaching, teaching, healing, and carrying out other sacred roles, just like the male apostles.[2]

So Mary was not alone in her role as priestess. What is unique about her, though, is her special elevated status among the followers of Jesus. This is a far cry from the image of Mary that sticks with us now.

The unfortunate downgrading of her public persona took place slowly over time. Through her own intrepid exploration, scholar Ally Kateusz informs us that "scribes and artists gradually changed their portrayal of Mary from an arms-raised liturgical leader to a silent woman who physically expressed her submission by looking at the floor."[3] I find this maddening and saddening.

Let's again call to mind the holy women in the Hindu tradition known as the Bhairavi Matas, the high female saints, the enlightened souls who have had a special connection to the Divine Mother. The identities and images of many of these women over the centuries have been guarded for a variety of reasons, but they are there.* In understanding that Mary was herself a Bhairavi Mata, we bring her further into the light as a very real living woman. In this work, she is restored once again to her stature as a holy woman with lifted hands and eyes who accomplished great things in her own ministry.

MARY AS HIGH PRIESTESS

One place where we see the remarkable position Mary held among the apostles strikingly conveyed is the apocryphal Gospel of Bartholomew, mentioned in chapter 4. This gospel provides several surprising descriptions of Mary's position in the early community that formed around Jesus's life, work, and resurrection. Again, the text may have originated in the second century, which means that it was written relatively close to the time of Mary's life—thereby suggesting that it indeed depicts authentic material about her.

One passage in Bartholomew shows her inviting the male apostles to draw together to set holy space only to find herself embroiled in a debate as to who should lead the prayer. It's a contest of humble wills.

---

*According to Cindy Lindsay, some modern Bhairavi Matas have been identified, including Serada Devi (wife of Ramakrishna), Matta Jii (with Maha Avatar Baba Jii), Hasrat Bhaajan, and Bhairavi Brahmani, who taught Ramakrishna. (Personal email from Cindy Lindsay, February 14, 2020.)

The men say she should lead, Mary defers, and they in turn give reasons why they should not. Among the men who persist in denying this privilege to themselves is Peter, which is unusual on two counts. One is that he is the acknowledged "chief of the apostles" and usually ends up leading the prayer or song of praise. The other is that he is notoriously depicted in the gnostic stories as not being too keen on female authority, as evidenced by his belligerence toward Mary Magdalene.* Here in Bartholomew, Mother Mary is eventually persuaded to accept the honored position. She stands up before the men, spreads her hands to heaven, and offers a long holy utterance praising the Divine. We see in all of this that Peter and the male apostles hold her in especially elevated regard—and that she has no problem moving into the role of the high priestess.

Mary further springs to life as a spiritual leader in other texts written about her, such as, again, Maximus's *The Life of the Virgin* as well as the East Syriac *History of the Blessed Virgin Mary*, the West Syriac *Life of Mary*, and a collection of more than sixty different apocryphal manuscripts known as the "Dormition" narratives (stories about her special "death passage"). Picture Mary wielding an incense boat—a censer—to bring a fragrant scent into spiritual gatherings. This was a ritual action she took into her own hands—which put her on par with Hebrew priests, the only ones authorized to use this instrument in preparation for prayer.† In one manuscript she even instructs others, namely, the apostles, to set out the censer, which specifically tells us that she is their figurehead and mentor. Elsewhere we see her putting on special clothing before making an offering of incense to the Divine, clearly an action that affirms her status as a priestess.[4]

---

*On Peter leading prayer see Kateusz, *Mary and Early Christian Women*, 7; *The Life of the Virgin*, 136–37, in Shoemaker; and Bible Probe, *Transitus Mariae*, paragraph 10. For Peter opposing Mary Magdalene, see Pistis Sophia, 36, and Gospel of Mary 9:4.
†See Luke 1:8–11, Exodus 30, and Leviticus 16:12–14 for examples of the function of burning incense and/or using the censer being the privilege of male priests.

Another text adds a further dimension to our understanding of what she was doing by noting that on one occasion "a scent of myrrh went up, which the Lady Mary had thrown on the censer, and its odour went about all the regions of heaven."[5] This shows us that incense was considered a means of connecting oneself and those gathered with the divine realms, and that Mary was seen as a full-blown ceremonial leader whose holy power could be felt beyond this world.

These details also invite us to look anew upon the gifts of frankincense and myrrh made by the *magoi*, the holy men, at the birth of Jesus. Might such gifts have been intended not only to honor Jesus, but to pass the power of the high temple priests to Mary herself? Perhaps they even served on a practical level as resources to be used for her ministry, a private stash she could draw on to enact her authority and ritually commune with the domains beyond the earthly.

Mary's great authority as a high priestess and leader is affirmed in what's known as the *Six Books* narrative, where we once again see her praising the Divine in ceremony and burning incense to foster communication with the higher realms. But in this account, we see her in a much bigger way. She does more than just lead prayer—she preaches the word of Jesus. This is Mary the teacher.

Here we also see astounding aspects of Mary that surely no one ever heard about in church: she heals with her hands, exorcises demons, and "seals," (baptizes) people (which we will look at in more detail shortly).[6] She is shown to be a healer in the East Syriac *The History of the Blessed Virgin Mary*, as well.

Even more remarkably, we learn that she is a master in raising up the dead (the yoga known as parakaya pravesh). Her means involve using Jesus's swaddling bands from infancy, his bath water, or his body. She draws on these sacred currencies not only to bring two dead boys back to life, but also to perform an impressive list of feats, including performing several exorcisms, curing three cases of leprosy, reversing an act of sorcery, and healing two young men of infections. Again working with water in this way is a clear demonstration of siddhic powers over the elements, which Sri Kaleshwar says both she and Jesus had developed through reciting mantras, drawing yantras, and other practices.

Mary as ceremonial priestess, healer, death reverser, and even exorcist? How can it be that this information has been freely accessible to us all these centuries, yet in modern times all we are left with is an image of a Mother Mary with a very constricted role, a Mary with barely a history, barely a personal will, and barely a significance aside from her obscured participation in the conception of Jesus? This great cover-up has done us all a great disservice.

MARY AS AN ELEVATOR OF WOMEN

There is yet more to learn about this remarkable holy leader. The Gospel of Bartholomew gives us further clues about Mary's role in the holy community by looking at various interactions that she has with the apostles. In one significant encounter, Peter again shows up as her admirer. He insists that she be the one to ask her resurrected son Jesus to reveal "the things that are in the heaven."[7] This honor belongs to her, he asserts, since she possesses a more elevated holy status. Mary repeatedly tells him, though, that he himself should be the one to initiate the inquiry.

In this communication we see Mary as a teacher of a new way of being. By encouraging Peter to voice his question directly to their ascended master Jesus, she is instructing him in something unusual in the context of Jewish religious culture: a nonhierarchical way of relating. She is teaching here that all of us are equals both with those we consider divine (in this case, Jesus) as well as those we consider to be holy human beings (herself).

Mary then does something particularly striking for the times in which she lives: she specifically affirms the equal position of *women* in holy leadership. We hear this in the declaration she makes to Peter: "In me the Lord took up his abode [in other words, was conceived and birthed through her] that I might restore the dignity of women."[8] With this stunning statement, she is proclaiming that it is time for all women to be raised back up to their rightful place of power.

This is not the only time we hear Mary described as a model for women's elevation and liberation in early Christian texts. A writing attributed to Demetrius, the third-century Archbishop of Antioch, says: "Hail, Mary, through whom and by whom all the women in the world have acquired freedom of speech with her Lord!" Later, in the early fourth century, the poet Ephrem the Syrian writes: "In Mary there has come hope for the female sex: from the insults they have heard and the shame they have felt she has given them freedom."[9] Feminism was nearly two thousand years off, and yet Mary was already leading the charge.

There's more. If we look closely at *The Life of the Virgin*, particularly where Maximus describes Mary's mindful participation *in every moment* of the Passion, we can see that she endures the very sufferings her son experiences in parallel fashion, if not even more intensely. Through the power and wisdom she embodies throughout this ordeal, she is shown to hold a role equal to that of her son as a world-server who has come to release humankind from its suffering and karma. In Mary, the feminine is restored to its empowered place on earth and in all of Creation. And with her, all women are resurrected.

MARY AS TEACHER AND MENTOR OF WOMEN—AND MEN

As we have seen, Mary was a member of sacred communities her entire life. From the time of her infancy, she was always surrounded by supportive women. In chapter 3, I noted how she was tended by virgin priestesses starting at six months old, and how she continued her early life with such women in the temple. I also discussed how Elizabeth, whom the Islamic tradition states was Anne's sister and therefore Mary's aunt, was a supportive mentor to Mary when she was in the early stages of her pregnancy. My imagination gets piqued every time I think of the two of them spending those three months together, sharing their thoughts and prayers as divine birth priestesses.

Mary's role working in a spiritual community continued well beyond her birthing of Jesus. The apocryphal gospels tell us that she gathered sacred women to herself throughout Jesus's entire ministry. The canonical Matthew 27:55 also affirms that there were "many women" who followed Jesus and provided for him, but what we don't hear there is a detail we find only in *The Life of the Virgin*. There Maximus tells us that Mary "was the leader of them all, their source of support and their mediator with the Lord her son." He later repeats this idea even more pointedly: "[Mary] held authority: as the Lord did over the twelve disciples and later the seventy, so did the holy mother over the other women who accompanied him. . . . The holy Theotokos [her title, meaning "Mother of God"] was the leader and director of them all." Further on, he reports that she was involved with their "care and supervision," and that "she encouraged them and was Jesus's surrogate in their labor and ministry." She even took charge of the female disciples at the last supper, serving in parallel fashion to Jesus during this critical event.[10]

Mary as the leader of all of the women of the early spiritual community around Jesus? And Mary holding a "women's last supper"? That's deep. Moving, deep, and thrilling. This affirmation of her very great power and authority is nothing less than a validation of the powerful capabilities of women, writ large.

We also learn from the apocryphal documents that because Mary was so close to Jesus, she was the principal authority of his word before and after the crucifixion. As Shoemaker notes, *The Life of the Virgin* clearly shows us that by virtue of her strong connection with her son, she had "uniquely authoritative knowledge of his teachings."[11] And what exactly were those teachings? According to Maximus, they were all the things we would hope and expect: "love of God and humanity, compassion, benevolence, and sweetness, peace, humility, and patience, honor and obedience to parents, fasting and prayer and every other good work." And Mary gave these concepts more than lip service. She taught them "first by deeds and then by words."[12] In our present era in which many gurus have fallen off their pedestals and become abusive in one way or another, it is comforting to think that this great holy female teacher known as Mother Mary actually walked her talk.

Maximus also affirms Mary's remarkable courage and strength. He reports that she remained steadfast as a leader even when the other followers of Jesus dispersed in fear after his arrest. According to his narrative, she was the only one to stick with him from the time he was seized by the authorities through his internment and resurrection. Although a handful of his followers were present for the crucifixion, even they fled in terror, leaving Mary alone to sequester her son in the tomb by enlisting the help of Joseph of Arimathea. Again, as Maximus tells us, *she witnessed the resurrection itself*—unlike Mary Magdalene and the other women who accompanied her, who found only the empty tomb later on. In fact, according to Maximus, it was Mary herself who was the first to announce the resurrection to the apostles.[13]

This is in dramatic contrast to what we hear in the New Testament, which credits Magdalene as the source of this information. As we have seen through the teachings of Kaleshwar, it would make sense that Mother Mary was the first to convey the news of the resurrection because in fact she *orchestrated* the entire process through the yogas she had developed with her own Holy Womb Chakra. All of these striking depictions of Mary's towering strength and sophistication have frustratingly been erased from canonical accounts and therefore from our reality . . . until now.

Mary's leadership in the community progressed, and after the crucifixion she immediately came to serve not only the women, but also the men—among them the twelve male apostles themselves. In the oldest version of the *Six Books* manuscript, another venerable text whose reliability is suggested by the fact that it, too, may have been written as early as the second century, Mary is presented as the supreme teacher of teachers in the post-resurrection era.[14] This means she was the first head of the entire Jesus movement—a huge fact that has gone absolutely missing from modern Christianity. Yes, just as conveyed in various paintings of the "Madonna of Mercy," it was under Mary's cloak that the entire early "church" was housed.

This narrative even tells us that a divine messenger gave Mary a book of mysteries and told her to pass it on to the "apostles." What were those "mysteries," I have wondered? Again, the canonical Matthew affirms that women numbered among such "apostles." Another reputable source verifies that Mary indeed gave sacred books specifically to female evangelists so that they could take them and use them to deliver spiritual teachings in Rome, Alexandria, Athens, Beirut, and Thessalonica.[15]

All of these sources are talking about the existence of an entire early priestesshood, mentored by Mother Mary!

In *The Life of the Virgin* Maximus, too, provides several striking descriptions affirming that Mary was the centerpiece of the early and expanding Christian spiritual community. He reports that she initially set out with the apostle John to serve as a traveling minister but was turned back by a divine message to stay rooted in Jerusalem with James, the "brother" of Jesus, who was appointed bishop there. It was from that base that she imparted teachings to the larger Jerusalem population on matters of right living, including those regarding fasting and prayer. She also sent out male and female disciples to preach across the ancient world. Picture them returning to Jerusalem every year at Easter to report what they had been doing and to receive direction and good counsel from her. In this way Mother Mary was the anchor who supervised everyone's teaching and was nothing less than the chief mentor, guardian, and guide to these fledgling spiritual acolytes and instructors.[16]

This Mary is hardly the passive girl who allowed the Divine to have its way with her, as we've been brought up to accept. This is a mature woman with gumption, courage, intelligence, and leadership capacities that we've never been told about.

What's more, being the closest living embodiment to Jesus, Mary was the source of great comfort to the early teachers of the ways. This was particularly important given that, due to religious persecution, some of them were subject to harassment, confiscation of their property, and even death. She showed great care for their well-being and offered them much verbal encouragement not only about their ministries, but about the spiritual promise that those teachings offered them personally. Mary's kindness extended well beyond her students too. As Maximus states, "her mercy was not only toward loved ones and acquaintances but toward strangers and enemies, for she truly was the mother of the merciful one."[17]

Is this not the type of strong female role model that any woman— or, really, anyone at all on the high-road spiritual path—would want to have?

The depictions in *The Life of the Virgin* of women coming to Mary from around the Mediterranean to learn from her are echoed in the Dormition narratives describing her passing from this world.[18] In the East Syriac *The History of the Blessed Virgin Mary* we likewise hear that after Jesus's resurrection, "Mary remained in Jerusalem, and she was in constant prayer in the cave in the grave of Jesus; and multitudes of women used to go about with her, and many sick folk were healed there."[19]

What we learn in all of these lesser-known sacred texts about Mary, then, is that she was a tremendously influential, tremendously spiritually adept, and tremendously powerful holy woman. I am so glad to know this Mother Mary at long last.

MARY'S CLOSEST FEMALE MINISTERS

The apocryphal texts reveal that the women who followed Mary included a special bevy of close attendants. We hear in *The Life of the Virgin*, for example, that after Jesus healed the apostle Peter's mother-in-law from a fever (Matthew 8:14–15), both she and Peter's wife became servants and advisors to Mary. (It's also interesting to note here the verification that the apostles could be married.)[20]

According to this same text a certain woman named Joanna also became Mary's disciple. Known to be "wealthy and honorable," Joanna renounced her property, husband, and children to serve by Mary's side.[21] Luke 8:3 gives us the specific name of this husband, Chuza, and tells us that he was a steward or manager of Herod. This would have been Herod Antipas, son of Herod the Great and the ruler of Galilee and Perea during Jesus's ministry. Given this younger Herod's massive power and reputed role in the deaths of John the Baptist and Jesus, Joanna's rebellious choice to leave her marriage despite the risk of retaliation by the very violent patriarchs she was associated with shows us that clearly Mary's lure as a spiritual teacher had a particular gravitational pull.

In the *Six Books* story we learn that Mary was also regularly tended by three women identified as "daughters of Jerusalem," all holy virgins. Like Joanna, these women had left their parents and siblings to minister to Mary, despite the fact that they were from wealthy and powerful Jewish families. All three of them dedicated their lives to the Blessed Mother and followed her wherever she went. As we will explore in chapter 6, they were also the primary ministrants in her death ritual. Both the *Six Books* and *The History of the Blessed Virgin Mary* even provide us with these virgins' names. One was Calletha, daughter of a disciple of Jesus named Nicodemus who helped deliver Jesus's broken body to Mary in the tomb. Another was Neshra, daughter of Gamaliel, the chief of the synagogue, at whose feet the apostle Paul was brought up. And another was Tabetha, daughter of a Greek kinsman of the king Arbolos and a member of the family of Nero Caesar.

The History of the Blessed Virgin Mary adds that in fact "there were many other women with Mary whose names have not been written down."[22] The thought that a wealth of women whose names have been erased followed Mary carries a potency, doesn't it? In all of these recountings we see that Mary attracted to her a new group of women from the elite classes who were willing to give up all worldly possessions, become holy celibates like herself and the temple priestesses who raised her, and serve her as their teacher. According to *The History of the Blessed Virgin Mary* these women were fiercely devoted to their beloved leader. They regularly accompanied her, saying, "We will not separate from thee, O Mary, blessed mother, except through death."[23]

In the Christian tradition we've been shown the image of Jesus with a devoted flock of followers and attendants, but never Mary. To my mind, these revelations from the archives and catacombs of time of a woman who walked in robes flanked by those who loved, tended, and listened to her are simply breathtaking. They carry a deep transmission of empowerment for all women.

Like the apostles depicted in the Gospel of Bartholomew, Mary's female acolytes were also curious about her divine birth abilities and would ask her, "How couldst thou conceive, and bring forth, without union with man?"[24] This shows us they knew she had teachings and trainings in this art that they had not been privy to, and they dearly wanted to know more. With Mary, these sacred women would also frequently "talk about the history of Jesus all day and all night long, and upon Him they used to meditate."[25] From this we can see that Mary helped them to understand the many angles of the events that had taken place. She took them deeper into the teachings and the practices that were not only Jesus's, but hers, as well. In the decades after Jesus's resurrection, then, it is clear that Mary became a guru of the next generation of virgin priestesses.

The discovery through this research that Mary was a supporter of women who wished to step up in their sacred roles has been a completely unexpected and meaningful revelation for me—as I suspect it may be for you, as well. The realization that she embodies not only Divine Love and Divine Power, but also the energy of "feminine mentor" makes me want to move toward her all the more. The knowledge that Mary is aware of women's struggles on the planet in this regard, and the fact that she is here for us, helps something deep inside me to relax. I have come to understand that Mary is not a "goddess out of time," but rather a Great Master who is intimately involved in our struggles. In terms of a go-to Sacred Female in times of need, it doesn't get better than that.

THE STUNNING FACT OF MARY'S BIOLOGICAL SISTER

This brings us to another overlooked detail, but one that we plainly find in the New Testament Gospel of John: the fact that Mary had a biological sister. John 19:25 tells us, "Near the cross of Jesus stood his mother, his mother's sister, Mary the wife of Clopas [sometimes written as Cleophas], and Mary Magdalene." It is unclear from this particular statement whether Mary's sister is being identified as one and the same with Mary the wife of Clopas, or not. Most people decide that two different women are being referred to here, for how could a mother name two of her daughters Mary? Yet the Gospel of Philip unequivocally verifies that the "third Mary" was the Blessed Mother's sister, stating, "There were three who always walked with the Lord: Mary, his mother, and her sister, and Magdalene, the one who was called his companion. His [sic] sister and his mother and his companion were each a Mary."*

And what of this sister, this third Mary? To find out more, we must dig into a couple of apocryphal sources. One is the Gospel of Pseudo-Matthew, which gives us another fascinating detail. It tells us that Mary "of Cleophas" was the daughter of Mary's mother Anne (Anna)—that is, she was indeed Mother Mary's sister. However the text here indicates

---

*Since we will hear shortly that that Mary's sister was indeed named Mary, we will assume that the scribe slipped in the second sentence, and that it should read "*Her* sister and his mother . . ." That said, however, Epiphanius, the fourth-century theologian, tells us that the previous wife of Mary's companion Joseph may have given birth to two daughters, and that one may have been another Mary (Kim, *The Fathers of the Church,* 144). These and others have been considered to be Jesus's siblings. Thus it would not necessarily have been incorrect for the text to read "his sister," but it would be inconsistent with the previous sentence.

that, in contrast to John 19:25, "Cleophas" (which we can assume was another spelling of Clopas) was not this "other" Mary's husband, but rather her father. Chapter 42 states:

> Jesus met them, with Mary His mother, along with her sister Mary of Cleophas, whom the Lord God had given to her father Cleophas and her mother Anna, because they had offered Mary the mother of Jesus to the Lord. And she was called by the same name, Mary, for the consolation of her parents.[26]

In other words this is telling us that Anne took a formal husband after her life with Joachim, a man named Cleophas, and had a child with him. The implication is that this occurred after Joachim's death, something that one of the manuscripts of Pseudo-Matthew confirms.[27] The passage also implies that after Anne achieved her miraculous parthenogenetic conception and birth of Mary, she gave birth through "ordinary" means and continued to be fertile well into even more advanced age, something I will return to a bit later.

Whether Cleophas/Clophas was in fact the husband (John) or father (Pseudo-Matthew) of this "other" Mary, taken together, these stories confirm that Anne was her mother. Therefore, one way or another, this Mary was indeed the Blessed Mother's sister. Pseudo-Matthew is telling us that the name Mary was "recycled" for Anne's second child since she could not fully complete the raising of her first one, whom she had given to the temple.

The matter of this naming becomes quite interesting if we look at *The History of the Blessed Virgin Mary*, which also tells us that Mary had a sister, but gives her a different name—Paroghitha, meaning "pullet" or "young hen."*[28]

---

*Note, however, that in this text it is Joachim (who here is called Yonakhir) who is the father of Paroghitha, not Cleopas. Note also that on page 92 the name is spelled Peroghitha.

Here's what I think happened. Anne probably initially gave her second daughter the name "Paroghitha." As a high priestess, Anne then raised this daughter to be a holy woman along the lines of Mary, although she did not train her to be a divine birth priestess or deliver her to the temple. I contend that, nevertheless, the second daughter began displaying the attributes of a "Mary," meaning a priestess of a particular type, as we will recall from chapter 3. At this point Anne granted her second daughter the *Mary* moniker (Maryam/Mariam/Miriam), *as a priestess title.* If we view the name *Mary* as a title for a woman of a specific holy order rather than a personal name, there is no problem in understanding why two sisters would be bestowed with it. Indeed this case of Anne's two daughters being given the same "name" is one of the strongest pieces of evidence that *Mary* was originally a priestess title.

I contend that both of Anne's daughters thus were part of the priestesshood I have identified as the Sacred Order of the Marys—again, the Sacred Order of Priestesses of Divine Love and Womb Mysteries. There were other named "Marys," too, who circulated in this ambit around Jesus—Mary Magdalene, Mary of Bethany, Mary the sister of Martha, Mary Salome, Mary the mother of James and Joseph/Joses (this was likely Mother Mary's sister[29]), Mary mother of John Mark, and Mary of Rome among them.* Let's also not forget the biblical high priestess Miriam, sister of Moses and Aaron, whose name, again, is the Hebrew equivalent of Mary. The fourth-century theologian Epiphanius even tells us that one of the daughters of Mother Mary's companion Joseph, by his first wife (therefore a stepsister of Jesus), may have been named Mary.[30] All of these Marys, I contend, would have been part of this priestess order—and I will discuss Magdalene's participation in it in what follows.

---

*For the mentions of Mary in the New Testament, see Bible Hub, *Strong's Concordance* 3137. Some scholars think that a number of these Marys refer to the same person. See, for example, Starbird, *The Woman with the Alabaster Jar,* 27, who equates Mary Magdalene, Mary of Bethany, and Mary sister of Martha.

MARY'S REMARKABLE SISTERHOOD
WITH MAGDALENE

And what of Mother Mary's relationship with her spirit sister, Magdalene? Writing in *The Life of the Virgin*, Maximus affirms what we hear in the canonical gospels, that Magdalene was a woman of "wealth and noble birth" who experienced a soul-level healing when Jesus cast "seven demons" from her. But he tells us more about the dynamic between Magdalene and Mother Mary than we find in the New Testament. Maximus outright states that Magdalene became a devoted disciple and "served Christ *and his pure mother* faithfully" (emphasis mine). Going further, he states that Magdalene became a "good and obedient companion of the queen, the holy Theotokos [the Blessed Mother], and she served as a minister with her."[31]

This tells us that as the elder Mary, a divinely born avatar, and thus the "Mary to surpass all Marys," Blessed Mother was a senior instructor to Magdalene on the teachings of love, compassion, womb mysteries, divine birth, and more. In other words, we can presume that Magdalene was not just receiving esoteric information, exorcisms, blessings, empowerments, and initiations from Jesus, but from Mary as well. Again, we hear nothing of this in the canonical gospels, yet it makes sense that Magdalene would have been instructed by the elder priestess of the tribe. This is a largely ignored point of discussion in the contemporary literature about Mary Magdalene—but an extremely important one to those of us who want role models for healthy relating among women of power in the spiritual arena.

The dynamic between the two women did not begin and end there. For we hear in *The Life of the Virgin* that Mother Mary essentially mentored Magdalene in developing her own spiritual capacities. Maximus states that "finally, [Magdalene] also became worthy of the grace of being an apostle, and she went about from city to city for Christ."[32] The implication is that it was Mother Mary who promoted her.

Maximus explicitly tells us that, as Magdalene's leader, Mother Mary sent her and those he calls "the myrrh-bearing women" to preach throughout the ancient world. "Myrrh-bearing" means that they were given the authority to use the censer in ceremony to set sacred space and communicate with the Divine, as Mary did—again, something that otherwise was restricted to male personnel in the Hebrew tradition. The term also indicates that these holy women were given the authority to anoint bodies with the aromatic myrrh oil at death as a method of embalming them and mitigating the odor of their decomposition.* Given that the fragrance of myrrh in censers was said to reach to the heavens—thereby connecting those inhaling it to those realms—I would contend that the use of myrrh on a body was also a means of helping the deceased person's soul travel through the otherworld. Thus we are being shown here that under Mary's guidance, Magdalene became a full-blown ceremonial leader and priestess of their conjoined ministry.

It was through this mentoring by Mary and the experience they gained by being out in the world that Magdalene and the other women became what Maximus identifies as "co-apostles" with the men. He states clearly that among the women, Magdalene held the same status as Peter did among men.[33] What we see, then, is that Magdalene rose in her position under Mary's tutelage to become the leader of the women's cohort, while Mother Mary served as the head of the *entire* early spiritual community centered around her and Jesus's teachings. Given that the rise to leadership in this community was probably not automatic among any of them, even the men, we can assume that after the resurrection, when Jesus was either no longer present as an earthly role model (canonical view) or had relocated to another land (Kaleshwar's view), Mother Mary continued to groom Peter in his role, as well.

According to these sources, the dynamic between Mother Mary and Magdalene did not remain strictly that of teacher and student, however.

---

*In *The Life of the Virgin*, for example, when Mary's soul leaves her body, it is anointed with myrrh by her disciples, presumably the women (Shoemaker, 136).

As we saw earlier in Maximus, Magdalene also "served as a minister *with*" Mary, which indicates a relationship between the two women that developed into one of equals. This ultimate equality is affirmed in *Philip*, where we learn that the Marys, including the Blessed Mother's sister Mary, were always around Jesus. John 19:25 further tells us that the Virgin and the Magdalene stood together at the foot of the cross during the crucifixion. Matthew 21:8 reports that Magdalene and "the other Mary"—here again presumably the Blessed Mother's sister—were the first to check on Jesus's grave. Again, while this is likely to have happened after Mother Mary completed her "womb yoga" work in the tomb to resurrect Jesus, it indicates the high status of both women, nonetheless.

These textual fragments imply that these great women must have operated together in a harmonious way. Even if Mother Mary ended up being the only one strong enough to be with Jesus every step of the way during the Passion, they all supported one another through the excruciatingly painful unfoldment of events around the crucifixion, and in their grief afterward, as best they could. It seems clear that they were united in mind and spirit around their mutual great work.

In fact, the role that Mother Mary, her sister Mary, and Mary Magdalene shared as constant companions of Jesus—and the fact that they all held the priestess title "Mary" (again, a moniker for their status as masters of Divine Love and the womb mysteries) affirms for us the idea that these three women were considered *the most advanced adepts* in this early community of committed spiritual practitioners. For only women of this caliber would be the ones to commune in the closest way with the divine avatar.

We would certainly expect nothing less of both daughters of Anne, who herself was an exceedingly high-level holy woman. Magdalene was, as well. I spoke of her rise through the disciples to the level of apostle. We further learn in the gnostic Gospel of Mary [Magdalene] that, as a woman of great spiritual perception and vision, she even became privy to special teachings from Jesus, which she then imparted to the apostles as a teacher among the men, as well. In both this text and the gnostic Pistis Sophia, Jesus powerfully makes a point of honoring her above all of the other disciples for her advanced spiritual understanding and purity of soul.*

THE MAGDALENE-MARY
CONCEPTION CONNECTION

I'd like to suggest here something more esoteric about the relationship between the Blessed Mother and Magdalene, one that specifically centers around divine birth. As we have seen, Mother Mary was a divine birth priestess. After scrutinizing gnostic texts related to Mary Magdalene, I have discovered evidence that she was, as well—though of a different kind.

To understand this, let's look closely at the Gospel of Philip 63, which describes Magdalene's relationship with Jesus and offers some other telling clues. There we find two sentences that the late great gnostic scholar Marvin Meyer says can be divided to read: "Wisdom, who is called barren, is the mother of the angels and the companion of [the savior]. The [savior loved] Mary Magdalene more than [all] the disciples, [and he] kissed her often on her [mouth]."[34]

This reveals . . . what? First of all, that 1) Jesus had a female consort, who was the Goddess of Wisdom known as Sophia, and 2) that he loved Mary Magdalene and kissed her frequently. Prior to this, in Philip 59, we are told that *Magdalene* was Jesus's companion. Basically, then, the gospel is telling us that Magdalene was understood to be one with Sophia—and the inclusion of "kissing" strongly implies that she was the love partner of Jesus.

The identification of Magdalene with Sophia alerts us to the fact that Magdalene is understood to possess certain very important characteristics of this wisdom goddess. In another gnostic text known as the *Thunder, Perfect Mind*, Sophia declares that she embodies a litany of

---

*For the exaltation of Mary Magdalene by Jesus, see Gospel of Mary 10, 18; Pistis Sophia 17–19, 87; Gospel of Phillip 59, 63–64.

opposite qualities—and here in *Philip* her duality as the "barren" one and birth-giving one is emphasized. This is significant for our understanding of Magdalene, because what is being pointed out is no ordinary birthing capacity. It is Sophia's ability to give birth to "angels" (high-level beings, or avatars)—again, manifestations of the Divine.

In other words, *Philip* is referring to the divine conception function of Sophia. This capability is something we see verified in the gnostic Valentinian creation story, where Sophia parthenogenetically conceives a girl child who is a kind of replica of herself. That child, known as the "Lower" Sophia, goes on to mate with a male consort to bring forth Ialdabaoth, the demiurge creator of the material realm.* If Magdalene is being equated with Sophia on the dimension of erotics and procreation, then she is being described as a female capable of achieving the same kind of high-level conception feats.

Again the tone and nature of Philip's declarations that Magdalene was the beloved consort of Jesus strongly suggest that their relationship was sexual in nature. A bit later in the gospel the text extolls the power of sexuality within a "pure" marriage. It's reasonable to propose that this reflects what was just said about Magdalene and Jesus, thereby suggesting that they were not just lovers, but that they were married. In several instances in this gospel, there are also references to the "bridal chamber" as a sacred place where a married couple can come together sexually, in purity—meaning, essentially, without negative spirits getting involved and exerting their influence. This "bridal chamber" seems to be a sacred domain, rite, or experience that brings the sexuality of two committed partners to its most exalted place.

When all of these references are taken together, the implication is that Jesus and Magdalene engaged in the "bridal chamber." In other words, they joined together sexually through rites of high-level sex magic. And their encounters produced "angelic" or exalted offspring.

---

*This story can be found in Irenaeus's tract *Against Heresies* 1.1–8.

This would perfectly correspond with my discovery that divine birth priestesses could be of two different types. They could either be celibates who conceived through sacred parthenogenesis, or high-level tantric priestesses who conceived through sacred marriage rites.* We know that Mother Mary was a specialist in parthenogenetic birth, as I explained in chapter 3. And, as I also mentioned there, she, too, was equated with Sophia. It seems that the Gospel of Philip is showing us that Magdalene was a "Sophia" whose divine birthing was accomplished not through sovereign parthenogenetic creation, but rather through sexual union.

That both the Blessed Mother and Magdalene, as virgin and tantrika, could be "Sophias" would not be a contradiction. It would be in alignment not only with the Sophia who reproduced through both solo (Upper Sophia) and partnered (Lower Sophia) means, but also with the Sophia who held things considered to be "opposites." In fact, in *Thunder, Perfect Mind*, this great female being outright declares: "I am the whore and the holy [one]."[35]

This may also well be the case because, in the depths of antiquity, the whore *was* the holy one. In the Hebrew Bible we find the qedesha, the holy servant of the temple who offered sex to men in what I contend was originally a highly meaningful spiritual encounter. In the Akkadian language of Mesopotamia she was the *qadishtu*, a sacred sexual servant consecrated to the goddess Ishtar. Further back, in Sumer, the term for this sacred woman was the *n u-gig*, and she was a high priestess/queen dedicated to the goddess Inanna. The title essentially meant "queen of heaven who is also a prostitute." I have surmised that such a priestess conducted the highest-level royal sacred marriage rites to engender divine offspring.†

---

*See Rigoglioso, *Mystery Tradition*, 13–18, for a discussion of these various kinds of divine birth priestesses, and 110–12, regarding the qedesha priestesses in the Hebrew temple, who are described as virgins yet also sacred sexual servants.
†See Rigoglioso, *Miraculous Conception*, 108–11, for a more in-depth discussion of these roles and related references.

In the Hebrew tradition the qedeshim, the plural term for the sexual servants mentioned above, were also "temple weavers," those very personnel who carried out the significant role of creating the huge veil that guarded entry to the holiest part of the temple. While these weavers were identified as being virgins, it seems they carried out sex rites—at least in some cases. I have argued that originally these women were trained to "weave" divine children into their sacred wombs, and in chapter 3 I made the case that Mother Mary was in this lineage—though, again, as a celibate. It seems Magdalene could have been a priestess in this lineage (or in a related lineage if she was not specifically a qedesha) as well, but, in her case, she would have been functioning as a tantrika.

What's important here is that "virginity" did not necessarily mean "abstaining from sexual union." It may simply have referred to an inner wholeness, a sovereignty arrived at when the person had achieved a certain level of inner spiritual unification.* Such spiritual mastery may, in fact, have been originally required for one to become a qedesha—thereby explaining how priestesses of this nature would have been designated as "virgin" regardless of their sexual status and practices. Certainly it would have been required of high-level practitioners of conception mysteries such as Magdalene and Mother Mary.

As I have discussed in *The Mystery Tradition of Miraculous Conception*, these sexual priestess roles were met with increasing disapproval by the religious authorities. They may, in fact, have also migrated from their original spiritual intention to offer petitioners an experience of unity with the Divine into more base exchanges of sex for money.[36] This state of affairs might explain why the woman in Luke 7:36–50 who anointed Jesus's feet with myrrh oil was portrayed as "sinful"—the implication being that she was a prostitute. The function of anointing with myrrh, as we have seen, was always a prerogative of sacred personnel only. So here in Luke we have the case of a priestess, who also seems to be a prostitute.

---

*A point also emphasized by Bourgeault, *The Meaning of Mary Magdalene,* 137–38.

In 591 when Pope Gregory said that Mary Magdalene, who is introduced in Luke 8:2, was one and the same with both this unnamed woman who anointed Jesus's feet and Mary of Bethany, the sister of Lazarus (Luke 10:39), he may not have been wrong. By connecting similar overlapping stories throughout the gospels, a cumulative argument can indeed be made that all of these instances are talking about Mary Magdalene.[37] Indeed, we learned earlier that Magdalene was a "myrrh-bearing" woman. The main problem here is in equating Magdalene's sexual priestess role with common prostitution and therefore sin. We see in Luke 7:36–50 that the Pharisee who hosted the dinner was already looking upon this woman negatively, so it's no surprise that centuries later, as the patriarchal control of the church had advanced, she was fully seen as the whore who was missing her spiritual aspect.

Thus despite the original sacred meaning of the "prostitute" status and the originally exalted meaning of "virgin," when Christianity framed Mother Mary and Magdalene as the passive, sexless vessel and the harlot, the virgin-whore dichotomy was born. It has stuck with us to this day, and only serves to oppress women further through sexually controlling stereotypes.

Did Magdalene fulfill her function as a priestess of "sacred marriage" whose role was to conceive an avatar? French legends tell us that at some point after the crucifixion, Magdalene left the Holy Land in exile with a "servant girl" named Sara Kali (sometimes written as Sara la Kali). Margaret Starbird suggests that this girl was actually the daughter of Magdalene and Jesus, and points out that her name *Sara* meant "princess" in the Hebrew tradition.[38] Based on the analysis of Savina Teubal, it seems clear that Sara/Sarah was in fact a priestess title.[39] *Kali* equates her with the Hindu Kali, the wrathful, dark, yet loving form of the Mother Goddess who takes on the torment of this world. Such sacred naming may suggest that the "servant girl" was indeed the divinely born child of Magdalene and Jesus's encounters in the sacred marriage bridal chamber. Alternatively, as mentioned in chapter 4, Kaleshwar maintained that the two were indeed married, that after the resurrection Magdalene joined Jesus in southern India and had children with him, and that their bloodline still exists throughout the world.[*40]

How does all of this expand our understanding of the relationship between Mother Mary and Magdalene? First of all, if Magdalene was indeed the wife of Jesus, then the Blessed Mother was her mother-in-law. This is certainly a fascinating idea that has been given little consideration in the literature on Mary Magdalene. To my mind this thought not only rouses curiosity about what that might have meant for their partnership, but it also offers a healing energy regarding the often uncomfortable dynamic between mothers and their sons' wives. Perhaps Mary and Magdalene provide an archetype of healthy relating for women in such a familial constellation, which often degenerates into tension, competition, and even abuse. The relationship between these two Marys is worth meditating on to explore that further.

Second, it's important to emphasize that Magdalene's name *Mary* is a sign that she, too, was a member of the specific order of priestesses of which the Blessed Mother belonged (and led). What I've shared above thus gives us a better picture of how these two special priestesses of Divine Love and womb mysteries were operating. These revelations suggest that they operated as a kind of divine birth "tag team." That is, (Mother) Mary served as the Sophia/Mary holy womb priestess who brought the avatar to the planet in a parthenogenetic conception ("weaving") rite, while Mary (Magdalene) served as the Sophia/Mary holy womb priestess who gave birth to his lineage of exalted children through sacred marriage/bridal chamber/tantric rites.

Might these two great women have been connected through previous contracts prior to their lifetime, then? Might they have agreed to come to the planet precisely at the same time to pulse the great ripple

---

*Theories have also been proposed that the child or children of Magdalene and Jesus could have been the ancestors of what eventually came to be the "first race" of kings in France, the Merovingian Dynasty. See Starbird, *The Woman with the Alabaster Jar*, 62–64.

of healing onto the planet through Jesus and a lineage they had high hopes for? What kind of conversations would they—and Jesus—have had over this? Could a bond deeper than any of us may have imagined been forged between these two women?

MYSTICAL ASPECTS OF THE "TRINITY OF MARYS"

Let us explore the relationship between Mother Mary, her sister Mary Paroghitha, and Magdalene. What I have been shown in a meditation with my colleague and friend Belinda Haverdill is that the three Marys worked together as a "trinity," and that in doing so they drew on the sacred geometry of the triangle in their spiritual work and in assisting Jesus. This is especially fitting given that the triangle has been one of the world-wide ancient symbols of the womb. So it seems that a "womb trinity" was needed around Jesus to hold or, at the very least, amplify the womb energies for him. As I discussed in chapter 4, these were the energies, Kaleshwar tells us, by which Jesus ultimately drew his power for healing and manifesting, the miraculous powers of the siddhis.

Belinda and I have intuited together that each Mary had her particular gifts. As we have seen, according to Kaleshwar, Mother Mary had already merged with Mother Divine during her pregnancy with Jesus, and was therefore a walking representative of this Great Goddess on Earth, transmitting her wisdom and energies wherever she went. Magdalene was deeply connected with the feminine sexual mysteries, being the probable sacred marriage partner of Jesus. She had also received further elevation of her status as a teacher from Mother Mary. What I also intuit is that Magdalene was—and still is—a woman who is nearing her own full merging with Mother Divine (again, what we could call her ascension). Unlike Mother Mary, who has completed the process, however, Magdalene may still be working at it on the soul level, and thus she serves as a kind of model for every woman who wishes to engage at these deep spiritual levels.

Belinda intuits that Mary's sister Paroghitha was very connected to the earth, a kind of medicine woman who aligned with the subtle angelic beings that I will talk about in chapter 7. What I sense about Mary Paroghitha is that, being the "least visible" of the three Marys, she represented the energies of gentleness, calmness, and, especially, humility, given that she was not destined for world fame like the other two (indeed, she's been nearly erased from the record). She held the quiet role in the shadows, without seeking glory.

My intuition also tells me that Mother Mary served as a spiritual teacher and role model to Paroghitha, as she did for the entire early community, and that Paroghitha is very much continuing on her path of reincarnation through a variety of lifetimes on earth. With each new incarnation, she is perfecting her spiritual growth in the way that her sister and Magdalene have done before her. Thus, on some level, Mary Paroghitha is even closer to those of us who are seeking awakening and ascension than Mother Mary and Magdalene, and can serve as yet another resource on the inner planes for those on the path.

Ultimately I envision that these three Marys were sources of mutual moral support and inspiration for one another. Although Mother Mary was the head of the community, she may have received teachings and insights from her sister and from Magdalene, as well, accepting them as sister gurus. The possible harmony among them feels deeply healing, offering an alternative to the energies of power struggle that can sometimes besiege spiritual sisterhoods. Perhaps you, too, will discern further information about these three women as you meditate with them and open your intuition about them.

THE POWER OF TWO

Returning to the earlier thread about Mary and Magdalene's special partnership related to divine birth, I have also received in medicine ceremony that these two women had their own special "power of two" and yin-yang energy dynamic that represented a unified whole when taken as one. . . . I see them, in fact, as two intersecting triangles, one pointing down from "heaven to earth" (Mother Mary) and one pointing up from "earth to heaven" (Mary Magdalene).

For this vision I was inspired by the teachings of the women of the Q'ero people of the Andes in Peru. According to the research of Maureen Walton O'Brien, the Q'ero see the female body as imbued with a three-dimensional sacred geometrical energy grid that they call the "Luminous Structure." This structure features two triangles of energy, one pointing down (its points at the two shoulders and just below the navel), and another pointing up (its points at the two hips and just above the navel). These energy triangles express the overlap of the heart and womb systems of the female body. Their intersection creates a diamond of energy around the navel that reaches up to the heart and down to the womb.* Students of Kaleshwar can discern that this diamond also incorporates an energetic point about an inch and a half below the navel known as the "nada bindu" point, which represents the point of power of the entire womb (and which is also present in men).

Looking at this schema from the perspective of the Mary triangles, we can see the downward facing one as representing the heart love energies of Mother Mary and the upward-facing one as representing the sexual love energies of Magdalene. These two aspects are meant to be integrated in the body, mind, and spirit of the woman for optimal, empowered functioning.

I believe that as we continue to reunite the heart and the womb energies within us, bringing together what was torn asunder in the creation of the virgin-whore dichotomy, we engage in a very great personal and collective healing work. As I see it, Mother Mary and Magdalene are supporting us in completing this great healing on earth at this time. This is why understanding how they literally worked together when they walked together is especially important, as it con-

---

*See Walton O'Brien, *The Good Darkness*, 72–73, for depictions of this.

tributes to our ability to foster the energetic harmonization of their qualities within us.

MARY'S "OTHER" CHILDREN?

Much has been made of references in the canonical gospels to Jesus's "brothers and sisters." Does this mean that Mother Mary had other children?

As a move into this discussion let's return to the detail in the Gospel of Pseudo-Matthew that offers a stunning glimpse of Anne and the implications it has for our understanding of the life of a priestess after she has conceived a child by divine means. The text tells us that Anne eventually had another child (Mary Paroghitha), and it strongly implies that this happened through ordinary means. To bring forth her second daughter, she was not alone in her garden conducting a conception ritual while her companion Joachim was off in the wilderness. Rather, it seems she engaged in sexual union. In telling us this, the author of Pseudo-Matthew indicates that "virgin birth" priestesses like Anne could be released from their celibacy vow and their commitment to sacred parthenogenetic conception after they had fulfilled their mission to bring an avatar to the planet.

The canonical gospels are ambiguous as to whether this was the case with Mary. Matthew 1:24–25 tells us that Joseph did not have sexual relations with Mary until after she gave birth to Jesus, as he was instructed by a divine messenger. This implies that he *did* eventually consummate their relationship. Matthew 12:46–47 and Luke 8:20–21 identify Jesus as having had "brothers" and Matthew 13:55–56 and Mark 6:3 even give us their names: James, Joses, Judas (or Juda), and Simon. Interestingly these two passages also tell us that Jesus had sisters—although, true to the patriarchal habit of disappearing women, they do not name them or tell us how many of them there were. I had to go to other sources to find out that there may have been two such sisters, and that they may have been named Salome and

Mary, Salome and Anna, or Assia and Lydia.* In some of the manuscript fragments of the Infancy Gospel of James/Birth of Mary we hear repeated the names James and Simon, and even Joseph (could this be the Joses of Matthew?). Given that the gospel recounts Mary's early life only up until the time of Jesus's birth, the presence of these individuals in the text indicates that they were already children of Joseph when he was assigned guardianship over Mary.

Church fathers and theologians have debated for centuries as to whether these "brothers and sisters" were indeed born of Mary, or whether they were children of Joseph by a previous woman. In another twist, some have argued that these children were born of Mary's *sister* by the aforementioned Cleophas/Clophas (identified in some accounts as the brother of Mary's guardian/husband Joseph). This would mean that these "brothers and sisters" were actually *cousins* of Jesus.†

While Pseudo-Matthew itself echoes that Jesus's so-called "siblings" were Joseph's children, not Mary's,[41] if we combine what that gospel says about Anne's sexual life with what the canonical gospels say about Mary's, we get a possible picture that divine birth priestesses eventually *could* go on to have normal sexual relationships and ordinary family lives. Of course, being such advanced spiritual women, their lives remained centered around the sacred, as we see with Anne, who persisted in raising a second "Mary" priestess, as well as with the Blessed Mother, whose life was dedicated to spiritual service.

My personal intuition is that while Anne may have gone on to

---

*Epiphanius said they were born of Joseph's previous wife and says they were named either Salome and Mary, or Salome and Anna. (Kim, *The Fathers of the Church*, 144). The apocryphal *History of Joseph the Carpenter* (2) names them as Assia and Lydia, also born of Joseph's previous wife. Many have also become familiar with Claire Heartsong's reports of the extended families of Anne, Mary, Jesus, and other figures in the Holy Family in her books, based on her work in trance states. Her information at times validates what is in the apocryphal, gnostic, and canonical gospels, at times contradicts it, and at times expands it.

†See, for example, Bauckham, *Jude and the Relatives of Jesus*, 13 onward, particularly those mentioned in footnotes on page 13.

have a sexual marriage and bear a child from it, Mary did not. I base this on the clues in the Infancy Gospel of James/Birth of Mary mentioned above, that Joseph indeed had at least one son when he met Mary, and possibly even more—including the gospel's very author, James. As I explain in what follows, I also draw from Maximus. I sense that Mary's purpose was to bring in the avatar alone, and focus her life on spiritual ministering.

Whoever the mother of Jesus's siblings (or close cousins) was, we naturally want to know how Mary related to them because clearly they became prominent people in her life. In *The Life of the Virgin* (which maintains that these children were originally Joseph's by another woman), Maximus offers an intriguing detail about their family dynamic that is not found elsewhere. Presumably working off other now-lost documents, he reports that when Joseph took the young Mary to his house after being assigned her guardianship by the temple (echoing what takes place the Infancy Gospel of James/Birth of Mary), he honored her in a most extraordinary way. He did nothing less than designate her "queen and leader," and he "appointed her over his daughters." Maximus goes on to tell us that Joseph also "appointed the Virgin Mary as the leader and teacher and ruler of all the members of his family, to instruct them as himself so that she would make his daughters wise."[42] Given that the Infancy Gospel of James/Birth of Mary clearly indicates that some of these children were male as well, taken together, these two narratives imply that Mary became quite the exalted "mother" of the entire household.

Mary's role is remarkable to consider, especially given that, according to the Infancy Gospel of James/Birth of Mary, she came to Joseph's house when she was possibly as young as twelve years old. How did these children, who were significantly older than she, receive her? Were they welcoming? Resentful? Was Mary's spiritual training in the temple adequate to help her in her new and very practical duty as a stepmother after living in a cloistered community among sister virgins? Apparently so, because Maximus says:

Although [these children] were older, Mary was distinguished by the grace of the Holy Spirit. But as the blessed and all-holy one was a treasure house of all virtue, so she also possessed meekness, tranquility, and humility especially. And most of the time she remained at the house and was devoted to prayer and supplication to God with great fasting and labor.[43]

Mary not only kept the peace and avoided conflict with these children, it seems that she also won them over on every level, including spiritually. For *The Life of the Virgin* tells us that Joseph's "sons James and Jude followed Christ as disciples, and his daughters became disciples of the holy Theotokos [the Virgin Mary]."[44] We also hear from various texts mentioned earlier that Mary was often present with the children said to be Jesus's "siblings," following him in his public gatherings. Given what a minefield a stepfamily situation can be (as I, and no doubt many others, have experienced), the fact that Mary was even able to attract some of these children to her ministry is an extraordinary feat indeed, a true testament to her own ability to apply skillful means in any circumstance, even the most potentially challenging.

Mary in fact may have been the very glue in a household divided over Jesus's ministry. While *The Life of the Virgin* implies that his stepsiblings were happy to serve him in his work,[45] the canonical gospels present a mixed picture as to the degree of trust they had in his miracles and teachings. In John 7:5 we hear that they "did not believe in him." Matthew 3:20–21 tells us that they felt he had "lost his senses."* Certainly it seems that at least one of them came around, however: after the crucifixion, when the apostle Peter left Jerusalem, it was Jesus's "brother" James who became leader of the church in Jerusalem and was held in high regard by the Jewish Christians.[46]

We can presume that, as in many families, Mary may have had to

---

*However the text is ambiguous as to whether it is Jesus's siblings or people in the larger crowd who are holding these views.

deal with a variety of familial opinions regarding a controversial figure who had emerged from within their own midst. As Jesus famously declared, "No prophet is accepted in his hometown" (Luke 4:24), and perhaps he was talking from personal experience here! Once again, it is reasonable to conjecture that this great woman met these differences with great wisdom, and that she inspired, if not unity among them, at least a manageable holding of differences.

Mary's "family" also grew beyond these stepchildren. In John 19:27 we hear the moving words of Jesus from the cross in which he "assigns" his beloved disciple John and his mother to each other as, henceforth, mother and son. We are told that from that day forward Mary lives in John's house. I agree with those who contend that this is further evidence that Mary's other "children" were really Joseph's—otherwise why would they not have automatically been the ones to take her in? Whatever the case, surely this gesture was Jesus's way of caring for his mother after his death by ensuring that she would be able to live with a person who would have no ambivalence about their teachings and would therefore be a better support to her in her life going forward.

The mother-son relationship between Mary and John was indeed borne out according to the apocrypha. *The Life of the Virgin* tells us that John lived with Mary in Jerusalem until he received the spiritual message to take her to the city of Ephesus (in modern Turkey). There he, Mary, and the female apostles continued to teach.* After John's death, James, in his role as the bishop of Jerusalem, took Mary back to that city and took care of her for the rest of her life.[47]

Mary as high priestess, wise mentor, and skillful family member is a whole new Mary we've never seen, one whom I've been delighted to introduce to you. Her restored image carries a potent medicine, does it not? This new view of Mary is only the beginning. There is much more for our

---

*Interestingly there stands in Ephesus a humble stone house that many believe to have been Mary's and that has become a destination point for devoted pilgrims and curious tourists since it was identified in the nineteenth century. For more on this see, for example, Ephesus, "The Virgin Mary's House."

world to ponder and receive in this regard, and I envision new insights, new discussions, and new realities emerging from this grand uncloaking.

CHAPTER 5 INTEGRATION ACTIVITY

The Marys, You, and the Women in Your Life

You're invited to take your Mary Journal and muse upon the following:

- How can you call upon Mother Mary to be your own spiritual mentor?
- What do you ask of her?
- What will you do to receive her messages?
- How does the thought that Mother Mary and Magdalene operated in cooperative sisterhood bring healing to your own life?
- Where do you need this kind of realignment, and how can you work with these two masters to shift your relationships with female family members or other women?

.... Online Guided Meditation ....

Divine Love with Mother Mary & Magdalene

In this guided journey, Mary and Magdalene attune you to their frequency of cosmic love. You will work with the symbols of the Mystical Rose and the Golden Chalice to help you open your Sacred Heart and the loving creation powers of the womb. Receive the special blessings of the Mary priestess lineage through the transmission of these two great masters. See page 150 to register for the free meditations.

CHAPTER 6

Mary's Full Ascension to Divinity

Wherever she may have spent her last days, according to apocryphal manuscripts Mary did not "die" in the way most people do—just as she was not brought into this world the way most people are. Texts that have come to be known as the "Dormition" and "Assumption" narratives describe her unusual means of leaving her body. This process was considered to be a kind of falling asleep, combined with the full "assumption" of her body into heaven. These events came to be honored as the Feast of the Dormition of Mary by the Eastern Church, and the Feast of the Assumption of Mary by the Western Church, both celebrated on August 15 each year.

To help us understand what is being described here I will focus on one such Dormition text, the *Six Books*, so named because its author says the apostles wrote six books about Mary's passing that they were to carry around with them as teaching aids. Six books—that's a lot to say on the topic! Clearly the events around Mary's dormition and assumption were abounding with information critical to the education of others about the nature of the spiritual realms and Mary's role in them.

William Wright brought this *Six Books* text to the attention of the modern world in 1865 when he composed an English translation of what is the second-oldest version of the Dormition manuscript thus far published.*[1] The narrative provides us with a description of

---

*Wright's translation appears as "The Departure of My Lady from This World" in *Journal of Sacred Literature and Biblical Record*.

something little explored that I would like to bring attention to here: the remarkable ritual that was conducted to help Mary's soul leave her body. I believe this was nothing less than a ritual to help her complete her spiritual ascension and apotheosize—that is, fully merge with Universal Divine Mother. In other words, this was the rite that helped her take her final step into becoming the Goddess that so many of us now know her to be. Indeed, this report is filled with remarkable happenings that give us a clue as to how six full books ultimately could have been written on the matter.

The date the document sets for Mary's dormition process can be calibrated to 33 or 34 CE, according to Wright.[2] Using 4 BCE as the commonly accepted year of Jesus's birth and assuming Mary was between twelve and sixteen when she conceived Jesus (as implied in the Infancy Gospel of James/Birth of Mary), the *Six Books* dating would suggest that Mary lived until she was anywhere between forty-one and forty-six years of age. This differs significantly from *The Life of the Virgin*, in which Maximus says she was closer to eighty years old.[3] Given the descriptions of Mary's extensive ministry and mentorship over the apostles as described in *The Life of the Virgin* and suggested in other apocryphal gospels such as the Gospel of Bartholomew, I am going to assume that Maximus was closer to being correct.

Let us turn our attention to the details of the Wright translation to give yet more flesh and color to the pale image of Mary that has been cultivated by traditional Christianity. As we explore what appears in this piece of writing, we'll get a much fuller understanding of Mary's enormous powers, and of what a master of her nature had to undergo in order to make the profound transformation from human to Divine.

In the *Six Books* story we learn that for years Mary had a practice of leaving her house every morning and evening to visit the tomb of Jesus, the entrance to which hostile religious authorities had blocked off with huge stones. According to the narrative, Hebrew priests, angry that she was leading people "astray" in her veneration of Jesus, had pressured her to cease her display at the tomb and either return to the temple and the traditional teachings of Judaism or leave and go to her home in Bethlehem.

Mary refused to stop her devotional practice—and this certainly presents a side of her that we have not seen so far: her strong will in defending her spiritual convictions. This is a far cry from the "let it be" girl of the canonical gospels. By this point, near the end of her life, she had clearly experienced the maturing and ability to say "no" that came from witnessing violence and experiencing tragedy.

Yet in this rendering we see that rebelliousness was still not natural to her, for the confrontation took its toll. Mary fell sick soon after this unpleasantness and decided go to her house in Bethlehem. The altercation disturbed her deeply enough to cause her to want leave not only the region of Jerusalem but the very earth plane itself. She had finally had enough of this very challenging world, and she wanted to move on to greener pastures.

Mary invited the three virgins who attended her—named, as we will recall, Calletha, Neshra, and Tabetha—to go with her, and all of them willingly agreed to join her and care for her on this journey. Perhaps, as Maximus suggests in *The Life of the Virgin*, there were still others who were part of the retinue whose names we do not know.

On the night she and her holy virgins arrived in Bethlehem, Mary felt especially unwell and called her attendants once again to bring her the censer of incense so that she could pray to her son's soul. Her prayer was that Jesus would send the various male apostles to her bedside to minister to her as she left her body. This tells us that she had the power to prophetically foresee her own impending passage out of this world, an ability attributed to various holy people throughout history.*

We can augment this episode with some bits from *The Life of the Virgin*, where we hear that Mary's foretelling of her own crossing was owing to a communication from the archangel Gabriel—the same

---

*Examples include Lahiri Mahasaya and Paramahansa Yogananda. See Blackman, *Graceful Exits*; Yogananda, *Autobiography of a Yogi*, chapter 36; and Yogoda Satsanga Society of India, "Final Years and Mahasamhadi."

being who had announced that she had conceived a child. According to Maximus, Mary's death was heralded when Gabriel granted her "the sign of victory" in the form of a date palm branch that he handed her. As the author explains, this was "in order to show that she had been victorious over every order of nature."[4] The conferring of the date palm was therefore affirming of what we have already learned from Sri Kaleshwar—that Mary had mastered the elements and had acquired the totality of siddhic powers and the full range of abilities conferred through atma kandana yoga (taking one's soul out of the body and then returning it) and parakaya pravesh (bringing the dead back to life). These indicated her special mastery over even the realm of death. Here we are seeing that her skills would be applied not only to Jesus's resurrection, but to her own ascension as well.

Mary's assembling of the other leaders affirms her role as the key figurehead of the early Christian community. It indicates, too, that she knew this process would require special ritual attention. In this, I propose, she was preparing for the end-of-life ceremonial death rites that I believe were necessary for a priestesses of divine birth to ascend to her next stage as a full-fledged divinity who would no longer incarnate on the earth plane. We see this dramatically played out in what follows.

According to the Wright translation, each apostle received a message on the inner planes and was brought to Mary's side through "clouds of light."[5] Given that they were in far off places like Ephesus, Rome, Jerusalem, and India, their miraculous transport suggests they possessed the power of "sky walking," a siddhic practice recorded in ancient stories by which holy people have been known to propel themselves through the air across great distances so that they could convene.* We hear that even two of the dead apostles were brought to her, suggesting that Mary was communicating with both this

---

*As Keith Dowman writes, "The abilities of flying in the sky, walking through rock, or knowledge of the language of animals and birds, reading minds and so on, are powers that may be attained through a surfeit of merit and heightened awareness"; see Dowman, "Motivation of the Lay Pilgrim," from *The Sacred Life of Tibet.*

world and the realm beyond, as befits a holy adept of her nature.

A moving encounter took place as the apostles assembled around their great leader. As they approached Mary's bed, each one kissed "her breast and her knees,"[6] and knelt before her. This is an indication of the great authority she held in their lives and the tremendous respect and affection they had for her. Clearly the "breast" references her loving and compassionate Sacred Heart as well as her nurturing qualities as a mother. The "knees" represent her more human aspect, and the will with which she had walked the earth as an emanation of the Divine among the people. These apostles were honoring both Mary as priestess and Mary as woman. Occurring at a time when males dominated the sphere of traditional religious leadership, the apostles' gestures are a remarkable and unusual display of honor toward the feminine that clearly underscores Mary's status and stature.

Mary then uttered a surprising prayer. She asked the Divine to keep her opponents from burning her body when she was gone despite their disturbing threats in this regard. Clearly this indicates that the destruction of her body would have impeded the ascension process that we are about to witness, and that Mary was gravely concerned about this. This suggests that her death would be something along the lines of the "rainbow body" process attributed, again, to certain Buddhist adepts.* In such cases the body must remain available as it goes through a rapid decomposition until "rainbow lights" are seen above what was once its material form. The burning of Mary's body would have prevented her from completing this culminating moment of all of her lifetimes, and we can therefore understand why making sure this cruel act was not performed on her person was of utmost importance to her. In this detail we are thus being reminded of Mary's high pedigree as a divinely born human being herself, a true avatar.

---

*See, for example, Gyaltsen, *Heart Drops of Dharmakaya,* 135–37, and Holland, "The Rainbow Body," 6.

MARY'S HEALING POWERS GO ZENITH

The Wright manuscript tells us that following Mary's prayer, a series of fascinating supernatural events took place. First, a tremendous thundering and the "voice of a man"[7] were heard above her chamber. When the people in the surrounding areas noticed these signs, they recognized them as a spiritual call and invitation. Those who were deaf, blind, dumb, and sick began processing to Mary's house—all of whom were healed by her very presence. Women in particular, from many cities and regions, including Rome and Athens, came to honor her with gifts and offerings, and any with pain or afflictions were also automatically healed. Among them were two women with evil spirits, which Mary released by praying over them—once again demonstrating her skills as an exorcist.

By offering prayers or sprinkling water over individuals, Mary also cured a woman of leprosy, healed a woman afflicted with a painful bladder condition, and restored the sight in a woman's eye. And the healing didn't stop there. The narrative states that among the many afflicted who flocked to her house in Bethlehem, 2600 men, women, and children were cured by Mary from her deathbed as she prayed to Jesus and sent forth her helpful energy over the multitudes.

But trouble soon followed. When local judges and priests heard about these sudden healings, they sent a mob of some thirty men to take Mary and the apostles into custody. At this point, another unusual event took place: Mary and those ministering to her were lifted up, carried over the heads of the approaching men, and transported to Jerusalem. When the men entered her house in Bethlehem, they were shocked to find only empty rooms.

While this transportation detail may seem to be a fanciful Catholic insertion, a bit of fictional drama, it does have an echo in more contemporary "disappearance" accounts of groups such as the Native Americans of the Mount Diablo area in Northern California. In this case a legend relates that Spanish troops corralled a group of local indigenous people into a thicket one night, keeping watch until morning, when they intended to kill them. At that point, however, their plans were foiled. After seeing what appeared to be moving lights in various parts of the thicket during the night, the soldiers descended in the morning only to find the indigenous group gone—a phenomenon that left the military men bewildered and frightened.[8]

The moving lights detail indicates that these people were being supported by an otherworldly presence—much like Mary was with the thundering and unearthly sounds that seemed to emanate around her. In Mary's case we're definitely talking about an avatar who could communicate with beings of the interdimensional realms from the time she was a child, as we've seen throughout this book. For those of us open to such things, the idea that she would receive otherworldly assistance so that she could complete her ascension process and her contracted mission on earth at this absolutely critical moment in her journey is not too much to consider.

The account goes on to tell us that with Mary safely ensconced in a house in Jerusalem, news of the unusual events reached even the local people and so impressed them that the afflicted of the entire city put out a prayer to her for their healing. The resistance continued—as did the Divine support. When those opposed to her ministry attempted to burn her house down with everyone in it, a repelling fire issued forth from her door to frighten trespassers away before they could commit their deed. Interestingly this echoes another legend of Mount Diablo recounting that on one occasion a group of "bandits" distracted Spanish soldiers from pursuing Native American locals there, only to mysteriously disappear from sight into a mountain cave from which flames and loud roars were emitted.[9] Clearly these bandits were some "other" kind of allies to the indigenous peoples—beings also capable of mastering the fire element!

We learn from the text that at the miraculous sign of this fire in Mary's abode, the local judge in Jerusalem had a spiritual awakening. He suddenly recognized Mary's holy role and called for a stop to the marauders. Turning from those opposing Mary, he went to her house with his son in tow, asking her for the healing of the child's stomach and bladder aliments. He had recognized that a great healer was among them, so why not have her tend to his own very human needs? Despite her weakened condition, Mary stood with the incense censer before her, stretched out her hands, and prayed over and blessed all who were gathered before her.

The healing reached well beyond the town. As virgin holy women and apostles tended to Mary at her bedside, her spirit continued to perform spontaneous healings of people as far away as Rome and beyond. At that stage, her protective energies also emerged. She was said to have come "like the sun" to sailors in danger of shipwreck who cried out to her, and guided their vessels to safety. She rescued men who were about to be killed by robbers by rising upon them like a flash of lightning.[10] Mary also heard the prayer of a mother whose boy had fallen into a well and rescued him from drowning. The big and the small, crowds and individuals—all were served by Mary regardless of status, and she seems to have had a particular penchant for the common folk.

These depictions of Mary healing people clearly affirm what we saw in chapter 4, that in her adulthood she had developed from a holy maiden into a mature master who had cultivated a variety of other siddhic abilities in addition to being able to divinely conceive. We see from this description that, like many great masters recorded throughout history, Mary possessed the ability to heal through prayer, intention, and the laying on of hands. Her powers were so great that she was even capable of protecting and healing people at a distance. She was also able to "hear" the calls of others and tend to many individuals at the same time. This indicates that her consciousness had reached a very high stage of development such that it was empowered to travel out of her body and bilocate many times over.

The fact that Mary was perceived as "sun" and "lightning" indicate that her incredible light body was already fully activated, able to instantaneously wormhole its way through time and space. This is the very kind of potency attributed to holy people from time immemorial, and establishes Mary as not a fantasy figure, but rather a living Bharavi Mata, an avatar who was in the final flush of her lifetimes on earth. She had mastered the Holy Womb Chakra, had achieved the powers Kaleshwar tells us are possible through this process, and was ready to go out in a blaze and merge with the Light of Mother Divine.

MARY'S ASCENSION RITUAL

As described in the Wright translation, it is at this point that the ritual to assist Mary's soul in passing from her body formally began. The holy group ministering to her was given divine guidance to carry her, bed and all, from the Jerusalem house to an interesting location indeed—a place with three caves "and a raised seat of clay."[11]

This is a powerful image. First of all, in her being carried to a cave I contend that Mary was being returned to the sacred womb of Mother Earth, the very kind of power spot where she completed the process of divine birth by delivering Jesus, as we hear about in the Infancy Gospel of James/Birth of Mary (18–19). Here, at the end of her life, she was traveling to such a special location to have a divine death. Second the "raised seat" motif recalls the "throne" upon which the oldest version of the Infancy Gospel of James/Birth of Mary tells us she sat when she conceived Jesus.[12] At her death passage, this royal throne represented the new one that she would occupy as she underwent her transformation from human to divinity in her form as Queen of Heaven.

Once Mary was ensconced into this hallowed setting of Mother Earth, her disciples continued to care for her as she prepared to depart from her body. One very important thing to note is that while those ministering to her in her last hours are identified in Wright's manuscript as the male apostles, the oldest layer of the Dormition text originally depicted women, not men, around Mary's deathbed.[13] This means we can revision what follows as a purely female-centered rite being conducted by priestesses—which also corresponds with women's ancient role as the original midwives of the dying. This would particularly befit the ceremonial passing of a divine birth priestess who had been born of and raised by holy virgins. I believe that Mary's death rite was as much a "sacred mystery" as were the divine birth rites, and therefore that it, too, was for the eyes and ears of holy women—sacred virgins—only.

An echo of the "women only" aspect of the rite is still preserved even in the Wright narrative in its portrayal of the first ones to come to Mary on her final day on earth: Mary's mother Anne, along with her relative Elizabeth, and even Eve, who is identified in the text as "the mother of all human beings."[14] The fact that all of these women were themselves no longer on the earth plane underscores the idea that the veils between earth and the realms beyond were increasingly parting for Mary at this stage. This is something that, in fact, is not unusual for many humans in the death process, who typically report being greeted by ancestors on the other side. In Mary's case Anne put her mouth on her daughter's breast and kissed it, praising her and affirming that she had known Mary would be a vessel for the Divine from the time she was in her own womb.

Even in Wright's version of the *Six Books* it was not until these women honored Mary and congregated at the honored place at the head of her bed that the Hebrew patriarchs assembled around her. These included Abraham, Isaac, the prophets, and others—as well as, eventually, Jesus himself. The gathering of this retinue to assist Mary with her departure, including individuals who had themselves left the earth plane, was clearly taking place on multiple dimensions of reality. She had the support of the many who had understood her great role on the planet, and who wanted to see her succeed in her ultimate realization.

According to the narrative, Mary had her beloved avatar son place his hands on her eyes and bless her. Those gathered by her bedside (again, which we can imagine were originally only her female acolytes) asked her to leave them with a blessing too. The process of Mary's ascension was clearly a heightened time in which her powers were pouring forth, and her attendants surely did not want to miss out on her healing balm any more than the people of Bethlehem, Jerusalem, and beyond did.

The very final prayer Mary uttered while still in her physical body was delivered not just on behalf of the individuals gathered around her—rather, it demonstrated the role she would maintain in her ascended state for all humans as the great Mother of Mercy. She asked for something sorely needed on the planet: that the "bad times cease on earth"—including pestilence, death, captivity, the sword, and famine. I contend that she knew this would be a long-term process that would require patience, fortitude, and the full awakening of humanity.

I believe this is why, in the next breath, Mary also encouraged humanity to honor her. The deeper meaning of this, beyond any fragrance of Catholic propaganda, is that those who made the effort to connect with her essence would benefit from her healing energies and wisdom. She was clearly indicating that she was available to offer her gifts of illumination, and that this is what would bring about the great transformation of the earth plane.

In the account, Mary's blessings continued, becoming ever more specific. She petitioned Jesus to provide counsel to the youth and upliftment to the old. She encouraged him to heal the sick, relieve the afflictions of those who were suffering, feed the hungry, and free people from violence. With her special love for the sea and seafaring, she also asked him to protect all sailors and bring them safely home. Turning her attention to the fertile earth, she petitioned that the lands be saved from locusts, blight, mildew, and hailstorms, and that the fields be blessed and bring forth good harvests. She then prayed that "blessings and joys be on the earth forever and ever."[15]

Although the Wright manuscript indicates that Mary was placing the power to manifest all such things in Jesus, we can discern a deeper layer in which it is *she* who was the Divine Will and Power behind all such blessings. And her petition that all who call upon Jesus for assistance be filled with be peace and concord reminds us of her request that they honor her own Light, as well. I believe Mary knew in her final minutes on the earth plane that the invoking of the Divine Masculine and Feminine energies—and the calling upon of their healing powers—would be required henceforth if humanity were to triumph over the great challenges that had been beset upon it. These challenges had come at the bidding of the adversarial forces that she, her sacred relatives, and the entire early spiritual Christos-Marian community themselves had known so well and had come to the planet to redress.

At this point in the ritual, Jesus instructed not only the gathered disciples but "all created beings" to begin singing "with the voice of Halleluiah"[16] so as to usher the soul of the Blessed Mother out of her body. The moment had finally come. Mary, still alert, bid Jesus goodbye with cheerful affection. He then instructed the disciples to lift her into a "chariot of light," and we are told that they did so, bearing it to "the Paradise of Eden."[17]

In this breathtaking sequence of events we can see that the ministers in attendance (again, originally presumably all holy women) were engaged in a deep prayer to assist Mary with this energetic process. She did not do it or go it alone—just as Jesus had not been conceived or resurrected without the presence of extremely skilled holy women who were joined together to assist. Clearly we are being shown that the work of Mary's holy priestesses in this instance involved a specific visualization of light, and a sacred kind of singing or chanting that evoked the heavenly harmonies that Mary experienced during her divine birth training and her conception process.* They were engaging the song of the angels, the light language of the divine realms. Perhaps their chanting included what we would know as mantras.

It is only owing to all of this sacred tending that Mary was able to move into the "Paradise of Eden" on the other side of the veil, where Jesus restored her to life again. We can interpret the Wright manuscript to be showing us that she had achieved "Mahasamadhi," the conscious leave taking of the body that is accomplished only by very great adepts.

---

*See Rigoglioso, *Mystery Tradition*, 103–5, 131–32, for a discussion of the relationship of light and heavenly harmonies to Mary's conception of Jesus.

But the journey was hardly over. Jesus subsequently took her on a ride to the realms beyond. The first stop, we learn, was the "lower heaven," where Mary saw several "houses": that of ice, snow and frost; that of rain, dew, and heat; that of winds, lightnings, and blast; and that of clouds and whirlwinds. She continued on, ascending next to the "the heavens of the heavens and the waters above the heavens."[18] There she saw the heavenly Jerusalem where apostles, angels, ancestors, and other spiritual beings were present. Following this, she passed through twelve gates, at each one of which she was honored and praised by varying groupings of these beings and elements, as well as by the very moon and sun themselves.

What is this *Six Books* narrative telling us? Clearly Mary's ascension process was a profound initiation for her soul. As she approached her fully divine beingness she was moving further and further from the realm of the terrestrial "elements" (earth, air fire, water) and more and more into the domains of pure energy.

It is fascinating to note that Mary's "ascension through the twelve gates" is in direct contrast to the seven portals that the soul of the deceased human must go through as described in the gnostic Gospel of Mary [Magdalene] (9). There Magdalene shares with the apostles special teachings Jesus has given her indicating that the transitioning person's soul will encounter seven "Powers," also called "Adversaries." These forces include Darkness, Desire, Ignorance, Zeal for Death, Realm of the Flesh, Foolish Wisdom of the Flesh, and Wrath.

Magdalene reports that these Powers will challenge the soul, telling it that it "belongs" to them and will never escape their clutches. In order to ascend through each Power's gate, the soul must respond firmly by saying that it has released all worldly attachments, desires, and ignorance.

The reward for the soul in making this arduous journey successfully is to rest in Silence for one aeon—a very large stretch of time—presumably before it continues its journey. What we know from the Valentinian gnostic creation story is that Silence (Sige) is the original primordial mother Goddess who unites with the "Deep" (considered to be masculine), to create all of reality.* So according to these special teachings given by Jesus to the Magdalene, the human soul, in having been rebirthed into the realm of death, must re-gestate for a while in the womb of the Goddess.

Magdalene recounts in her gospel what amounts to Jesus's instructions governing the human's difficult—but needed—encounter with its own "Shadow" once its soul leaves its body. The Soul must reckon with any ways in which it has "missed the mark" in its lifetime by having fallen prey to any of the Powers, that is, the energies associated with our famous major vices. But, ultimately, it must come to an understanding that its nature transcends it errors, and it must remember who it truly is as a divine essence beyond the body and the personality. The Soul must stand up for itself, unequivocally, in the face of forces set to test it.

In the *Six Books* story, in contrast, we see that Mary apparently did not need to go through this kind of personal reckoning. This is, perhaps, unsurprising—she had already come into her body as a high holy being, and, as the narrative explicitly states, during her lifetime she had successfully "purified herself from all evil thoughts."[19] That is, she had done her best not to succumb to the vices of the human experience, and she had taken disciplined spiritual remedies whenever she stumbled. We are shown, therefore, that, unlike that of most humans, Mary's soul was granted immediate entry to the realms of the angels and masters. Wouldn't we all like that!

We see, however, that in her otherworldly ascension journey the Blessed Mother was not fully exempt from encountering the dark side—hardly. We are told that, with Jesus by her side, she witnessed "hidden and terrible things,"[20] and things that humans had not yet seen or felt but that they were being prepared for in their own ascension process. In Mary's case because she was seeing these things as a soul that had already worked out its own Shadow, she could look upon them with neutrality, and even mercy.

---

*See Irenaeus 1:1–8 for the details of the Valentinian creation myth, as well as the discussion in *Gnosticism*, 162–77, and Angeline Campra's feminist interpretation of this story in Rigoglioso, *Virgin Mother Goddesses*, 193–96.

Then came the part she had been waiting for throughout all of her lifetimes. Wright's *Six Books* manuscript tells us that Mary's soul finally experienced "glories," "miracles," and "hidden and revealed things." She was even granted access to "the extreme limit of all created things." From this profound vantage point, she was able to look upon the "two worlds," the one in which things pass away and the one in which they do not. In the eternal realm, she saw brightly shining lights and "mansions without number," a place that had a beautiful fragrance—redolent, perhaps, with the very incense she had sent forth in her prayers during her lifetime.[21]

The inspired author of this text is telling us here that Mary did not have to experience the intense difficulty most human souls must undergo upon leaving their bodies—which is to grapple with the hell realms. Nor did she have to "rest" in the womb of the Goddess the way most humans do. Rather, in this culmination of her soul's evolution through many lifetimes, she was transforming into her perfected state. She had no need to rest in the Goddess/Silence like most souls because she NOW WAS that very Goddess, that Queen of Heaven, that Sovereign over the Deep.

With this we see that Mary had accomplished her full ascension and her full apotheosis.

We can infer from this passage that Mary and Jesus had both been working with the life and death portals, bringing one another back and forth between the realms, and helping one another cross over into ultimate Divine Reality. For just as Mary brought Jesus into incarnation through her body, so she helped rebirth him after his crucifixion. In the *Six Books* narrative, we see that Jesus, working on the inner planes, was able to return the favor.

MARY'S CHALLENGING PROPHECY FOR HUMANITY

Although she had achieved Goddesshood, Mary's work was not over. The account tells us that after her welcome into the realms of Light and her surveying of the realms of Pain, the Blessed Mother then uttered a prophecy. She stated that there would be a time when the sun would be "dark at mid-day,"[22] a time of famine, wars, and earthquakes, when mankind would be warring and hateful, destroying the planet. Thus, despite her earlier blessings for the earth, from her new vantage point she saw that humans would continue to go through a tough time. She discerned that there would be forces larger even than her intention, will, and power that would attempt to keep humanity in a state of suffering.

Mary's description of earth in its time of travail is eerily similar to the scenario that has continued to endure over the past two thousand years. Indeed, the earth has been trembling, warfare has been taking place on outer and inner planes, strange sicknesses have been plaguing us, and we are continuing to destroy the planet.

But there is hope. The *Six Books* narrative concludes with Jesus affirming that people would be assisted in their crises. How? Once again, by calling on Mary for assistance.

The *Six Books* is not the only place where we hear about Mary's ascension. *The Life of the Virgin* also describes it, offering yet further interesting detail. We learn there that when Mary's soul left her body, her Jerusalem house and surrounding area were "filled by a waft of indescribable perfume," and that an "unapproachable light spread forth over the holy body."[23] In this account, Mary's body was anointed with sacred myrrh by the priestess attendants and laid in the tomb where she had instructed them to inter her. On the third day the apostles opened it to find her body gone, with only the burial wrappings and shroud remaining. The explanation given is that her body had been "translated wherever her son and God wished."[24]

The phenomenon of light and the disappearance of the body indeed call to mind something I mentioned earlier—the appearance of rainbow lights that have been reported hovering over certain Buddhist monks after their death, and the rapid, odorless, and sometimes complete disintegration of their bodies. Thus what we are hearing in the *Life of the Virgin* is that Mary did nothing less than experience *her own resurrection*, one that took her out of the earth plane and into the realms of

Divine Light. And, like her son, she would continue to remain available to all humans who wished to call on her for support.

What, precisely, can Mary offer us now from her position as a fully ascended being who has merged with Mother Divine? Healing, yes. Comfort, yes. Intervention on the doings of the earth plane when requested, yes. But there's more. I contend that although Mary came to the planet already as an advanced and special soul, she represents the possibility of awakening into deeper consciousness that is available to everyone. This is her invitation. We will explore this further in the epilogue.

CHAPTER 6 INTEGRATION ACTIVITY

Passage and Ascension

Here are some questions to spur your reflections in your Mary Journal:

- What does learning about Mother Mary's passage into higher dimensions at the end of her life stimulate for you?
- What does "ascension" mean for you, and is this something you want for your own life?
- How do you intend to cultivate it?

.... Online Guided Meditation ....

Drawing on Mary as Your Ascension Mentor

As we have learned in this chapter, Mother Mary achieved her full ascension, which marked the completion of all of her human lives and her unification with Mother Divine. In this meditation, you will call upon Mary to activate the ascension codes within you more strongly so that you may accelerate your own spiritual growth and ability to come into One-ness with the Divine. See page 150 to register for the free meditations.

CHAPTER 7

Mary's Connection to the Subtle Angelics of Nature

Mary is a bridge to many worlds. As I mentioned at the beginning of this book, she is a rainbow connector by which people of many cultures may experience the grace of healing, the warmth of mother love, and the wisdom of greater realms. By sharing these commonalities through one multi-colored Goddess, people can see their unity with one another.

Mary also bridges us with our very own earthly logos. As a manifestation of Mother Divine, Mary is in fact intimately merged with the consciousness of the Goddess known as Gaia, our terrestrial home. Boring down further, Mary is therefore also one with Mother Nature herself. This is why her visions and prayers at the hour of her ascension were strongly focused on the well-being and travails of both human beings and the natural realms. And, as we have seen from Sri Kaleshwar, her intrinsic unity with the manifest world was in fact what prevented her from being able to rise up as the warrior to protect it. She had to leave that role to the masculine.

This understanding of Mother Mary as being one with nature is reflected in the connection that has been made over the centuries between Mary and the flowers of the natural world. In medieval and Renaissance Europe, nearly every flower imaginable had a second, spiritual name related to her, or an association with her qualities or life events. As Vincenzina Krymow writes, "Early Christians believed that fragrant flowers reflected Mary's spiritual sweetness, soothing and healing herbs reflected her heavenly mercy, while bitter and sour herbs mirrored her bitter sorrow."[1]

Some plants were dedicated to Mary because they flowered around the time of one of her feast days or at various special times of year, which, again, showed an understanding among the people of her interrelatedness with the seasons and cycles of nature. Most famously, stories connected her with lilies, roses, and violets, which were seen as symbols of her virginity, her divine conception capacities, her inner beauty, and her humility. But there was also a wide variety of other flowers related to the many moments and moods of Mary. There were those associated with her visitation by Elizabeth, like the columbine; those connected to her pregnancy, such as the forget-me-not; those tied to her flight into Egypt, like the clematis; and even those representing her qualities as a homemaker, like lavender and the marigold.*

What's the deeper meaning here? Flowers are understood to be manifestations of the beings of the subtle realms known by many names, but most familiarly referred to as the Fae or Faeries. Through my own work in expanded states of consciousness, I have come to understand that flowers literally are the third-dimensional expression of these beings, who largely reside in realms of reality beyond what we can discern with the five senses—again, sometimes known as fifth dimensional reality (or higher). When people expand their awareness through meditation, dreams, or sacred medicine experiences enough to see these beings as they truly are in those dimensions, such entities appear differently, less as form and more as diffuse beings of light.†

Thus equating Mary with flowers demonstrates a deeply felt human understanding, even if an unconscious one, that Mary herself is intimately connected with the Faeries. We see this association, too, at places

---

*See Krymow, *Mary's Flowers*, for a comprehensive and fascinating catalogue of the flora associated with the Blessed Mother.
†See Cromby, *The Gentleman and the Faun*, 23–26, for further discussion of this concept, and explore the images in Froud (*The Faeries' Oracle*), for example.

like Lourdes, which author Graham Hancock notes was a "fairy cave before Catholicism adopted it." Yes, he reports, "when little Bernadette Soubirous experienced visions in front of it in the mid-nineteenth century, she initially described the female figure she saw not as the Virgin Mary, but as *un petito damziella*, 'a little lady'—a term redolent of the fairy lore of the Pyrenees."[2] Whether or not Catholic authorities edited Bernadette's story to swap Mary for Faerie, what we're seeing here is verification of a deeper understanding that Mary and Faerie are one.

Mary as a Faerie? How can this be? What does this mean, exactly? Does not attempting to equate her with fictional beings diminish her?

This is not the place for a debate about whether Faeries are real or not, any more than it is the place for us to determine whether Mary herself is real or not. What I can bring to this discussion are several decades worth of substantive research and experiential exploration into these topics. This study leads me to proceed from the assumption that both Mary and the Faeries are "real," that both are here to help humanity, and that both may be accessed for teaching, guidance, and support on the inner planes of reality.

Proceeding from that possibility, let's take a look at what seer David Spangler has written about both Mary and the Faeries. In what follows, he refers to the Faeries with their oldest name known in Ireland: the Sidhe (pronounced *shee*), which means "people of peace."[3] The following remarkable quote is taken from a conversation on the inner planes that he had with a particular Sidhe being who has befriended him, known to him as Mariel:

> Many of us are more aligned with the feminine side of the Sacred, and of these, there are those who respond to the Light of the Marys. The "Marian" line of energy and service is actually older than that which manifested through Jesus and extends back into the time when our races were still one. It is a line of energy of which I am a part. Indeed, there is a legend among us that the Mother of Jesus was of our lineage, that the blood of the Sidhe ran in her veins so that Jesus became in his personage a reconciliation of our two peoples.

The Light and Love of Christ works for the wholeness of all, so in this sense it does bring our worlds together, and in our work, we seek a comparable objective. So we would see your Christ as our brother and co-worker. And as I say, there are those among our people who would seem Christ-like to you though they do not carry the mantle and the burden of planetary redemption and wholeness.

We recognize and honor the Christ in your lives, and to the extent Christ is a spark that lights the flame of your own sacredness, we are a breath to nurture that flame.[4]

Spangler goes on to write, "About two hours after receiving the above, while I was out for a walk, Mariel came back with a postscript":

There are those among us, very ancient even for our race, who remember the man Jesus and may even, if I am not mistaken, have interacted with him. The story I am told is that he was a man not unlike us in some ways, a man of joy and attunement to the world around him, particularly in his childhood and youth. Some of us, I am told, even acted as guardians of his well-being. This is not surprising. I have already told you of the tradition among us that his mother Mary was of a Sidhe lineage herself, so Jesus would have had Sidhe blood within him if this tradition is correct—and I believe it is. But he was primarily of your race for this is what his mission demanded. He was a crossroads in whom many "roads" of consciousness and life met and were brought into connection and wholeness, for wholeness is the essence of redemption, as I have said.[5]

In personal correspondence with me, Spangler elaborated upon the above:

I think the salient point here is that Mariel is recounting a tradition of which she is aware—and one in which she believes—that Mary was part of a Sidhe lineage, though this would not make her a Sidhe herself. It would be a line of energy, perhaps even a bloodline, that carried certain Sidhe qualities.

What is important to realize is that this is my translation of what she was telling me. "Lineage" was the word I chose to capture the sense of connectedness and participation that she was trying to convey, that Mary was part of something that the Sidhe also are part of, at least some of them. But this is different from saying that Mary herself (much less Jesus) was a Sidhe being, which is not what Mariel was saying. There is a current or line of energy representing certain sacred qualities and energies that is embodied by the various "Marys" of the bible—Mary, the Mother, Mary Magdelene, etc.—and by other women which is also present within the Sidhe world. In this sense, I suppose it would be like saying that a woman is a nurse. There are Chinese nurses and American nurses, but being a nurse transcends nationality. To say a woman is a nurse doesn't also imply she is Chinese or American. So a being—Sidhe or non-Sidhe, human or non-human, man or woman—may be part of this "Marian" current and thus related, the way all nurses are related to each other.[6]

What we can see from this wisdom stream is that it is more correct to look at Mary and Jesus not so much as Sidhe/Faerie beings, but rather as beings who possess *qualities* that are Sidhe/Faerie-like. This in and of itself is a powerful thought.

WHAT ARE MARY'S SIDHE/FAE QUALITIES?

Let's look at the characteristics of the Sidhe so as to amplify our understanding of Mary as seen through this facet of her crystal. First, the Sidhe have long been identified with the radiant light of Spirit through the old Irish title sometimes given them: "the Shining Ones."* David

---

*See Cromby, *The Gentleman and the Faun*, 23–26, for further discussion of this concept, and explore the images in Froud, for example.

Spangler's Sidhe guide Mariel affirms this aspect of Mary—and all of the holy women in her retinue who bear her priestess name—when she speaks of the "Light of the Marys."

Putting our attention on this Sidhe quality allows us understand that while Mother Mary may have roamed the Earth in a three-dimensional human body, she also radiated the light-stream substance of Creation to a greater degree than most people. Perhaps this was even manifested outwardly in her physical appearance as a glow of vitality. We can imagine that in carrying and emanating this quality, Mary was (and still is) a model for how we may activate and enhance what is referred to as our "light body." Such activation is known to be a process of spiritual evolution in which one's energy field expands to encompass and connect with the energies of the universe. As John White explains,

> According to many esoteric traditions, as we awaken to our oneness with God, bodily changes occur, most dramatically in the higher phases of enlightenment. In the final phase, the body is alchemically changed from flesh into light, becoming immortal. Enlightenment becomes a literal fact through the transubstantiation of flesh and blood into an immortal body of light. Various traditions have different names for this transubstantiated form, including the light body, the resurrection body, the solar body, and the diamond body.[7]

This understanding helps us recognize to a greater degree than ever before how Mary is an intimate champion of humanity's healing and spiritual awakening. She encourages the expansion of consciousness far beyond what is typically thought possible in ordinary third-dimensional life. Indeed she is all about helping people to achieve their own God/dess Self.

The Sidhe are also imbued with a profoundly caring attitude toward the Earth and all of her forms and creatures, and they hold a focus of service on their behalf. Some even contend that the Sidhe are angelic architects of the world of flora, and that, therefore, the Faerie beings expressed as the flowers and plants are emanations of them, lovingly tended by the Sidhe. Seeing Mary as carrying these Sidhe qualities helps us understand her even more deeply as being part of the very fabric of Mother Nature herself. We recognize the great degree to which she is nothing less than a major guardian of the Earth plane, a "mother" who supports the well-being of all planetary creatures.

As Spangler wrote to me, the Sidhe are characterized as well by "certain sacred qualities and energies," including peace, harmony, compassion, and love. This "current or line of energy," he affirms, "is embodied by the various 'Marys' of the Bible . . . and by other women." As we have learned, the very name that was passed down to us as *Mary* probably comes from the Egyptian *Meri*, an honorific priestess title that meant "beloved of, loving, lover, and the one who is loving." Spangler and his guide Mariel are indeed emphasizing that Mary and the Mary priestesses are part of this Sidhe-like lineage of women steeped in love.

Again, the love intelligence that the Marys carried also includes the mysteries of the Holy Womb Chakra and divine conception. I have come to understand that this is indeed a very important aspect of Sidhe/Faerie reality on earth. Let's follow this trail. First of all, in addition to the evidence for divine birth as a practice in various lineages of kings and queens throughout Western antiquity, including Egypt,* we also find it in the historical figures of Guinevere and Arthur. These I identify as the last legitimately divinely conceived queen and king, whose conception stories I alluded to in chapter 4 and will discuss a bit more later in this chapter. According to the deepest level of their history, they were also known to hail from early Sidhe/Faerie lineages that dwelt upon the earth.† Yes, there were humans who were also "Faerie"— and the "Avalon" stream of these two famous people was part of that.

---

*For divine birth in Egypt, see Rigoglioso, *Bearing the Holy Ones*, 70–94.
†See Berg, *Red Tree, White Tree*, 45–84, for an extensive discussion of this. This information is also developed in the course Heal Yourself and Our World by Reclaiming Guinevere, Arthur, the Fae, and the Round Table, accessible online through Seven Sisters Mystery School.

Thus acknowledging Mary's womb mastery as connecting her with the realm of the Fae allows us to see an expanded picture of both Mary and the divine birth tradition—one that bespeaks of a much larger interdimensional history than we have previously recognized.

The Sidhe/Fae are also known for their aliveness, and for their strong feminine energy. When we see Mary from this Sidhe angle, the dour, neutered image of her that we've been served transforms into one that is sensual, creative, light-hearted—and even imbued with a love of dance. Dancing is a huge Faerie occupation, as lore surrounding them will attest.* I have been shown that the Irish jig, in particular, was originally a Faerie dance, especially beloved by them because, for such beings (who always have "one foot" in the other dimension), the jumping associated with "jigging" allows them to soar up to great heights.†

Mary dancing? Is there evidence for this? Yes! In the Infancy Gospel of James/Birth of Mary, we are shown that Mary danced on the steps of the temple as a very young child as part of her initiation into temple life. I contend that the virgin priestesses who tended her up to that point taught her such sacred dances.[8] This tells us that, for Mary, dancing and spirituality go hand in hand. What a wonderful healing concept for those of us brought up in a Christianity devoid of this art.

As many of us know, Faeries love magic, mischief, and revelry too. Awakening to this Sidhe side of Mary allows us, among other things, to more fully appreciate her request for Jesus to turn water into wine at the wedding of Cana (John 2:1–12). Clearly she was asking for a wee bit 'o Fae magic in that—magic that was intimately connected to the power of sacred and fragrant intoxicants of the ancient world, no less. In turning to the Spirits, she was setting things up for everyone present to

---

*See Cromby, *The Gentleman and the Faun,* 32, for a description of the raucous Bacchanalia that are Faerie gatherings, and Froud, *The Faeries' Oracle,* 25–27, for a discussion of Faeries' connection with singing and dancing.
†The recommendation was that if you want to dance the jig like the Faeries, do it on a trampoline, and then you'll get the sense of what the Sidhe experience! They say they admire the humans who can jump high, like the folks in the Irish troupe Riverdance.

experience Faerie reality more exultantly themselves through expanded awareness, amplified heart connectivity, heightened merriment, raucous laughter, and, again, unbridled dancing. Rock on, Mary!

FAERIE MARY AS A BRIDGE BETWEEN PAGANISM AND CHRISTIANITY

Many of us have not known how to reconcile Christianity with the Sidhe/Faerie tradition, which is connected to the pre-Christian past in Europe, sometimes referred to as "Paganism"—and which has its counterpart throughout many cultures of the world. It has seemed that these two streams of spirituality couldn't be further apart. But as we are seeing here, for those who have favored the nature-based old religion, or who have rejected Christianity for its dismissive treatment of women, seeing Mary in her Fae light allows an embrace of her as a welcoming and safe female mentor. By the same token, for those ensconced within the Christian tradition, understanding that Mary's link with flowers has basically been an acknowledgement of Faerie reality within the church itself for centuries serves as an entrée to see her in a more expanded, empowered, and delightful light.

With this cross-bridging comes a deep healing. It brings together worlds within and without that have been torn asunder. When author Jeremy Berg first informed me at a conference in 2019 about the connection David Spangler had made between Mary and the Sidhe, I welled up with tears—which made his own eyes brim in recognition as well. When I presented a workshop on this topic at the Fairy and Human Relations Congress in June 2019,* the response was similar. People in attendance were deeply, deeply moved.

The stunning possibility that Mary and the Faeries are in some senses *one* is a large step for humankind in restoring what some are calling the "New Earth." This refers to an illumined way of living that

---

*Now known as the Gaian Congress.

carries the memories and energies of previous epochs on the planet in which life was more harmonious. It is characterized by a consciousness that fully acknowledges the reality of the Subtle Beings and the natural world, and is in co-creation with them. And, according to many, it is where we are headed.

Hundreds of years ago, the twelfth-century German mystic Hildegard of Bingen had already come to understand the link between the energies of nature, the fertile (hence, feminine) aspect of the Divine, and Jesus. This was expressed in the concept she frequently referred to as *Viriditas*, denoting the greening power of the Divine. Viriditas was characterized by freshness, fertility, and growth in the spiritual life.* Hildegard was not only a nun, she was a plant medicine woman—essentially an ally of the Faerie realms. I would guess that the altered states she experienced in which wisdom poured from her, which she recorded through writings, songs, and art, were stimulated by the psychoactive substances she knew how to prepare and administer. You can't get more Fae than identifying the Divine with the green of nature, and it seems Hildegard had an intimate, experiential understanding of this connection.

This "greening" of the Divine also links Jesus to the pagan figure of the Green Man, a Sidhe-type being who represents the cycle of new growth that occurs every spring. The image is in direct contrast to the dying Jesus on the cross. As a someone filled with Viriditas, Jesus is the tree that lives, not the tree that has died. We can see that the early Celts retained this understanding by including portrayals of the Green Man on their church walls, and by situating such churches near ancient wells and springs rich with flora.

Seeing Jesus and Mary as Faerie allows us to perceive them in their flush, verdant form. We can bypass the dead corpse version of a religion that we have been served, and we can see, embrace—and better emulate—their juicy vitality.

---

*For a discussion of Viriditas, see, for example, Reenu and Jones. Interestingly my last name, Rigoglioso, means "lush, flowering, or blooming"!

These understandings bring Mary and Jesus alive for us in our present day. Such insights tell us these great beings are not dried bone relics who can only be accessed through certain belief structures, the sterile scriptural lines of ancient manuscripts that are incomplete or have been tampered with, and stultifying rules that have been established around them. Rather, recognizing Mary and Jesus as carrying Sidhe energies lets us see them as living, breathing, continuing, moving, and growing intelligences who are here with us.

The reconciliation of Jesus, Mary, and the Fae comes through embracing their living, not their dying. The crucifixion drama can be seen to contain a strong subliminal message: anyone who crosses the line of knowing and bringing forth esoteric mystical truths and teachings will die, and in a horrible way. The reconciliation is in the healing that arises from bringing together what never should have been separated to begin with. Drawing the connections between Mary and the Faeries unites Pagan and Christian, and unites the ancient earth-based wisdom and emerging New Earth understandings. Given this, we might even see the work to bring humans back in touch with the Sidhe valence of Jesus and Mary as being part of the evolving Christos–Marian enterprise itself.*

MARY'S CONNECTION WITH THE UNICORN

We can't talk about Mary and the Faeries without looking at her association with the creature known as the Unicorn, the horse-like animal featuring a single horn protruding from its brow. It's worthwhile exploring this connection, too, as it reveals yet more about Mary's link to the mysteries, her role on Earth, and the relevance of all this to us today.

---

*Those wishing to hear and experience more regarding the connection between Jesus, Mary, and the Faeries may enjoy the audio workshop Jesus & Mary as Sidhe Beings, recorded at the Fairy and Human Relations Congress June 19, 2019, and available online at Seven Sisters Mystery School.

Lore, imagery, and natural histories around the world have abounded with varying depictions of animals identified as Unicorns for more than a thousand years. In the ancient Greek bestiary known as the *Physiologus*, the Unicorn is described a strong, fierce animal that can be caught only using a virgin maiden as bait. According to this text and other related writings spanning into Christiandom, the Unicorn can be beckoned only by a young virgin (or can be led to her by someone else), whereupon it will leap with glee into her lap. There it will suckle her breast, and she may peaceably deliver it to its intended captors.[9] In medieval times in Europe, the Unicorn came to have a particular identity and form as an elegant, white, horse-like animal with a long, tapered horn emerging from its head. This image persisted in heraldry and art of the period and seems to best capture the mystery of this being.

Like many individuals going back to ancient Greece, including various naturalists, royal personages, and explorers traveling around the world, our friend Hildegard of Bingen had no problem considering the Unicorn to be a real animal. She writes, "The unicorn . . . eats clean plants. In moving it has a leap, and it flees humans and other animals, except those that are of its kind, and so it cannot be captured. It especially fears a man, and shuns him. . . . but follows a woman."[10]

She, like many writers, extolled the healing powers of the Unicorn and its body parts, recommending shoes made of Unicorn leather to support healthy feet and even providing a recipe for Unicorn liver mixed with egg yolk as a cure for leprosy.[11] She matter-of-factly reports that the Unicorn maintained its powers by annually visiting the land that contained vital waters of paradise, and by eating the plants there.[12] Others writers specifically talked about its horn, asserting that the animal could dip it into poisoned waters to purify them for the safety of other creatures wishing to drink.[13]

The reliability of writers such as Hildegard gives us pause when it comes to dismissing Unicorns as simply the product of fiction, creatures that exist only in the form of rainbow-colored stuffed animals made for the amusement of young children. It seems there is a deeper story here, just as there is regarding the Sidhe—and regarding Mary herself. The many seriously produced and held writings and images throughout the ages reveal that the Unicorn seems to hail from the very world in which we find the Fae—the intersection of the third dimension and the realms beyond this one. This creature sometimes has been spotted in our own reality, where it has been manhandled, as we shall see, but it mainly seeks refuge in the inner domains.

Eerie possibilities abound particularly when we consider that beautiful horns claimed to be those of the Unicorn were kept in places like the treasury of Saint-Denis in Paris, the church of San Marco in Venice, and the royal treasury of Westminster Abbey in London. They were also incorporated into royal objects such as swords and cups, sometimes offered as significant gifts among the aristocracy, and some of which can be found in museums and personal collections to this day.[14]

These publicly appearing horns are now claimed to be nothing more than the very long tusk of the narwhal, a species of whale. However, back in the days when Unicorns were reported to be alive and well, these kinds of items were believed to be authentic. In addition, they were reserved for only select audiences.[15] This fact, and the magic attributed to Unicorn horns, leads one to wonder whether horns that were decidedly non-narwhal were indeed floating around in secret collections. Given the lore around the Unicorns, it would be reasonable to assume that such items, whether authentic or only believed to be authentic, were highly prized occult ritual objects. Thus with the Unicorn we are in the realm of the Mystery and high magic.

The mystery deepens and is compounded as we consider the long-standing special affinity between the Virgin and the Unicorn, which underlies its association with Mary. The capture of the Unicorn by the Virgin Mary became a popular image in Christian art, and illuminated manuscripts and stained glass in various churches featured Unicorn imagery.[16] Drawing upon the mystical motif of the Unicorn leaping into the lap of the Virgin, Christian writers as far back as the early centuries of the Common Era saw Jesus as the "spiritual Unicorn" who dwelt in the womb of the Virgin Mary, was slain, and was reborn.[17] Art from the Middle Ages often depicted a Unicorn and a maiden to represent Christ and Mary at the Annunciation, in particular. The maiden and the Unicorn were featured extensively on large woven tapestries that hung in the homes of the rich and famous of the era.

Given the elevated spiritual energy attributed to the Unicorn, the story of its hunt, murder, and resurrection as depicted in gory detail in one still-existing series of tapestries strikes the viewer as particularly shocking and sad. Among the rare remaining weavings with this theme, these huge, meticulously threaded panels are housed at the branch of the New York Metropolitan Museum known as the Cloisters, located in Manhattan. They were created probably in the southern Netherlands, around 1500, when, as former Cloisters curator Margaret B. Freeman affirms, "everyone believed in the existence of this marvelous creature."[18] The panels take the viewer through scenes in which the Unicorn is pursued by a hunting party like a stag, further lured by a virgin, chased to exhaustion, and mercilessly pierced with swords as it struggles, tongue lolling, to escape. Its lifeless body is finally draped over a horse and presented to the noble couple of the castle.

Some contend that the depiction of the brutal death of the Unicorn in this series represents the crucifixion of Jesus, who was also hunted, pierced, tortured, and killed at the hands of humans. The personages featured in this series, as well as the original commissioners and owners of these works (and of other related weavings), were members of complex, powerful royal and noble lineages of France that eventually bled into other European countries, as well. These families may have been associated with the crusades, chivalry, and possibly even the Knights Templar.*

---

*For the ownership of these tapestries by the Rochefoucauld family, see Freeman, *The Unicorn Tapestries*, 44, 46, and Boehm, "A Blessing of Unicorns," 25–28. For more on the lineage of the Rochefoucauld family, see Geni website, "Jean I, seigneur de La Rochefoucauld"; Brittanica, "La Rochefoucauld Family"; Office de Tourisme website; and Lindahl. For more on the possible connection of the royal Merovingian lines of France to a bloodline of Jesus and Mary Magdalene, see Starbird, *The Woman with the Alabaster Jar*, 62–64, 67–71.

In the early twentieth century the tapestries captured the attention of a member of one of the world's wealthiest families, who purchased them, funded their housing at the Cloisters, and visited them regularly.[19]

Those who trace the bloodlines of the elites and the various doings attributed to them might have their ears pricked by such associations. If the story of the hunt has any reality on the material plane, the images show that the Unicorn was coveted and pursued in acquisitive, avaricious, and perversely violent ways, possibly for the harvesting of its potent body parts. Even having its image adorn stone walls in palaces and fine homes was important, I would imagine not merely for decoration or insulation against the cold, but for the powers it transmitted.

WHY VIRGINS AND UNICORNS?

To my mind, the connection between the Unicorn and the Virgin points directly to perhaps the most "hidden in plain sight" aspect of the occult meanings surrounding this great creature—and the relationship of all this to Mother Mary.

It was the "purity" of the virgin maidens that was used to lure the Unicorns so they could be trapped. This points to more than the girls' sexual chastity; it recognized a certain refined spiritual nature present within them. Hildegard affirms that such female Unicorn allies were imbued with a "gentle and sweet" disposition, and adds another detail: they had to be "nobles."[20] Not all virgins or noble girls are nice, so, in my view, she was talking about a special breed of maiden: one who was of high pedigree, virgin, and possessed of elegant soulful qualities.

As I have noted elsewhere, this type of exalted maiden was none other than the *parthénos*, as the word appears in the ancient Greek texts. Parthénos denoted more than a mere virgin. It was a title that recognized a young girl, or even an older woman, as a priestess of divine birth.* Such a female had the power to give birth to avatars—representations of the

---

*For an extensive discussion of this, see Rigoglioso, *Cult of Divine Birth*, 39–43.

Divine who would dwell among us on the earth plane. She was highly trained in this art, highly spiritually enlightened, and highly sought after—at times as a prized commodity, like the Unicorn itself.[21]

Thus, in connecting the dots of all of these associations, we can determine that the Unicorn was intimately related to divine birth priestesses, miraculous conception, and resurrection through the womb. This, I contend, is why Mary, as the biblical parthénos par excellence, was so strongly associated with these illuminated horned beings. But while she was the most famous of such priestess, she was not alone in this great role. There were others, including, as I mentioned previously, women in high royal family lines the world over.* In Europe we see an example of one such priestess in the figure of the historical Queen Ygraine. The strangely reported conditions of her conception of King Arthur indicate that occult ritual magic was indeed involved in this process and, I would contend, that a deliberate divine conception was being sought after.† This role was enacted not only by enlightened women and lineages, but also by corrupted ones, with more nefarious consequences.†† In short, divine conception was a big deal among royalty, and this is why members of these families were so drawn to Unicorns and their associated virgins—especially the "Head Virgin," Mary. Their attraction to these creatures was thus marked by both awe and avariciousness.

---

*See Rigoglioso, *Bearing the Holy Ones*, 70–94 for divine birth priestesses of Egypt and 502–43 for mothers of Pythagoras, Plato, and Alexander as divine birth priestesses. See Rigoglioso, *Mystery Tradition*, 44–60, 113–20, for discussions of Mary's mother Anne, their relative Elizabeth, and the biblical matriarch Sarah as divine birth priestesses.

†This is discussed more extensively in the course Heal Yourself and Our World by Reclaiming Guinevere, Arthur, the Fae, and the Round Table, available online at Seven Sisters Mystery School. See also Berg, *Red Tree, White Tree*, 66–69 for details of Arthur's conception, and Rigoglioso, *Cult of Divine Birth*, 126, 75–77, and *Bearing the Holy Ones*, 512–15, for parallel instances of subterfuge in conception stories in Greece, indicating, as I have argued, that such descriptions thinly veil deliberate divine conception rituals.

††For corrupted historical figures said to have been born divinely, consider, for example, Alexander "the Great," (see Rigoglioso, *Bearing the Holy Ones*, 522–39) and Augustus Caesar (Seutonius, *Divus Augustus*, 95). For corrupted legendary figures, consider, for example, Perseus (Apollodorus 2.4.1), Theseus (Rigoglioso, *Cult of Divine Birth*, 75–77), and Romulus and Remus (Rigoglioso, *Mystery Tradition*, 81).

In understanding that Unicorns were affiliated with divine birth priestesses, we can recognize that sacred virgins did not willingly initiate any deception to trap these marvelous beings. Rather, their innocence was exploited by those in high places of power. Such duplicitous individuals would have been rejected by Unicorns, who were extremely suspicious of human males. Thus the exalted "lap"—the womb of the divine birth priestess where the Unicorn rested and suckled peacefully—could also be utilized by negative forces as a snare for the animal. Certainly Mother Mary experienced that reality when the particular "spiritual Unicorn" she brought forth from her womb quickly became the target of Herod's hunt soon after Jesus was born.

MARY OF THE TAPESTRIES

Mother Mary's presence is felt in the Cloisters tapestries in a number of ways. First there is the amazingly rich millefleurs design featured on the panels, in which scores of accurately depicted flowering and fruiting plants and trees abound. The majority of these plants indeed had readily identifiable medieval associations with Mary.* Thus the very background of these great works is the Faerie garden, Mother Mary's realm itself. Then, in one very damaged panel of the series, we have the literal appearance of the figure of the Virgin—the "Mary" stand-in—whose arm can be discerned circling the Unicorn's neck.

Finally we have the likely culminating scene of this drama with the "resurrected" Unicorn, whose broken body is now restored, but still imprisoned, as it sits chained to a tree. It is held within a circular fenced enclosure, once again in a field of Mary flowers. This field could be understood as the womb of Mother Mary itself, which, as we saw in chapter 4, was the portal by which the fatally wounded Jesus was brought back to life.

---

*See Freeman, *The Unicorn Tapestries,* throughout, and compare the flowers to the those listed in Krymow, *Mary's Flowers.*

The mystical connections between the Unicorn, the Virgin, and Mother Mary cannot be fully understood without looking at a set of complementary tapestries, made around the same time, which are located in the Musée de Cluny in Paris. In this series, the maiden and her relationship to the Unicorn is the primary theme uniting all of the wall hangings. And it is in the unfolding of the story from panel to panel that the relationship between the Virgin Priestess, Mary-as-Virgin, the Unicorn, and the relevance of all of this to our own lives, is revealed.

A seemingly different maiden appears in each panel, each one a young noble woman who is dressed in finery, pictured with aristocratic items, and sometimes tended by a female servant. We know that these maidens are virgins, because the Unicorn appears with each of them, and, in one scene, extends its front legs and hooves into the maiden's lap—a tableau that we have seen occuring only with chaste girls. Once again, the presence of the Unicorn plus the element of virginity straight away tells us these females are of the "elevated virgin" type—and therefore that they are in the "lineage" of Mother Mary as high queen of both virgin birth and exalted spirituality. This is an association we will see develop as the scenes progress. I will thus refer to each female depicted as a Sacred Virgin.

On the simplest level the Cluny series has been thought to express the encounter of the maiden with the five senses—touch, taste, smell, hearing, and sight. As Barbara Drake Boehm describes these scenes:

One lady touches the unicorn's horn; another takes a treat, perhaps something like a Jordan almond, from a golden dish; the third draws forth a sweet-smelling rose from a basket as a monkey sniffs another. In the fourth tapestry in the ensemble, the lady plays the organ, while in the fifth she holds up a mirror to the unicorn's gaze.[22]

There is a sixth panel, too, which art historians think may well represent none other than the "sixth sense," that of intuition. It is this culminating panel that, for me, serves as the clue as to how we may more correctly understand this entire series—and the more esoteric meaning being revealed as it relates to Unicorns, virgin priestesses, and Mother Mary's mentoring role in our own lives.

We begin this deep dive by noting that every Sacred Virgin stands or sits within the millefleurs design. This tells us that each one is situated within the "Garden of the Faeries and the Marys," and that the location of this drama is therefore the very place of the sacred womb. We are in the realm of the womanly mysteries, and what is taking place is a Feminine Mystery School initiation for those with eyes to see and ears to hear.

I thus suggest that in these weavings, the maidens depicted represent a single Sacred Virgin who indeed may experience something of a "journey of the senses"—but for a much deeper purpose than simply to enjoy earthly delights. The story being shown is one in which she receives an insight or gift delivered through each of the senses. The ultimate purpose of this journey is to have all aspects of her being opened sufficiently so that she may achieve full expanded consciousness and her ultimate connection with the Divine.

From this perspective, we can see that the first panel of the sequence is likely to be that in which the Sacred Virgin is about to eat something—the one commonly depicted as "taste." The young woman takes a single item between her fingers from a serving dish that is being offered to her by her lady in waiting. This is no mere dish; it is an ornate object, made of gold, almost in the shape of a chalice. The servant presents it to her in a reverent kneeling position. This gesture and the elaborate nature of the chalice tell us it must contain something significant to the Sacred Virgin. Perched on the Virgin's left hand, which she holds upright, is a bird.

Let's pause here to consider that according to the Infancy Gospel of James/Birth of Mary, the young Virgin Mary was trained in the temple where she "was fed there like a dove, receiving her food from the hand of a heavenly messenger." As I discuss in *The Mystery Tradition of Miraculous Conception*, this "food" was likely a sacred medicine or herb designed to help open her awareness to the interdimensional realms.[23]

Perhaps whatever the Sacred Virgin of the tapestries eats from this prodigious chalice similarly contains a substance worthy of mystical apothecaries such as Hildegard of Bingen, something that will begin to open her inner sight. This would be underscored if we considered the bird whose talons clasp her hand. While it has been variously identified as a "parakeet," "hawk," or "grouse," no one really knows what it is. It's not out of the question that it could be some form of dove—further underscoring the connection between the Sacred Virgin and Mother Mary.

The second step in the Sacred Virgin's journey is likely her playing of the pipe organ, accompanied by her female servant—the panel commonly titled "hearing." Now in her expanding state of awareness, she is no doubt being led further into the celestial realms through the harmonies of this instrument. We see echoes of this in Mother Mary's experience, again, in the Infancy Gospel of James/Birth of Mary, where we learned that the Virgin experienced the sounds of the "heavenly messengers" in her early training as a divine birth priestess.[24] We also saw that, during her ascension rite, divine tonings were engaged in to assist with her great passage from this world to the next. Thus harmonics are used to part the veil, and this, I believe, is why the Sacred Virgin is playing an instrument known to stimulate spiritual rapture—to the point where it was the main feature of cathedrals.

The third stop in the journey would then be the Sacred Virgin's sewing of a headdress of flowers, presumably for herself. This panel is called "smell," but what is sometimes overlooked in descriptions is that she is sewing flowers onto a headband. While they have been identified as either carnations or roses, the motif of the monkey sitting behind the woman and smelling a rose suggests they are probably the latter (although back in medieval times, carnations had a lovely fragrance too).

The headdresses the Sacred Virgin wears in all of the panels are quite elaborate, so why is she now constructing a simple floral wreath, the accoutrement of the country folk, many of whom still would have retained their pagan flair? I believe this indicates that she is entering into the Faerie realm, particularly as it is connected with Mother Mary, who was intimately associated with the rose as well as the carnation. In fact, beginning in the twelfth century, a garland of roses was originally called a "rosary"—a garland of prayers in honor of Mary.[25] This name was later transferred to the mala-like object used for reciting the Hail Mary and Our Father prayers.

Thus it seems our Sacred Virgin is creating a crown of Mary energies with which to adorn herself, one that suggests a Faerie folk "wedding headdress." With this she is further uniting herself with the heavenly realms of which the Blessed Mother was the renowned queen. This process would have been further assisted by the exquisite fragrance of the rose—scent being yet another doorway into inner mystical realms. The monkey in the scene, who is the only creature actually sniffing the flower, is telling us that this doorway can be accessed even by those of a seemingly lower order of consciousness—namely, most of us!

This brings us to a fourth panel, typically identified as expressing the sense of "touch," in which the Sacred Virgin gently grasps the horn of the Unicorn. This image tells us that now, presumably rather deeply into her expanded state of consciousness, she is coming into intimate relationship with the Unicorn who has journeyed on her left side throughout all of these sensorial stops. What is the Unicorn horn but the symbol of duality (the more typical two horns) having resolved themselves into a singularity protruding from its brow—the location of its own third eye, its palace of intuition and mystical seeing? As I have come to understand, conception by the divine birth priestess occurs when she has similarly achieved inner unity, in her case by uniting within herself the "opposites" of masculine and feminine.* The Sacred Virgin herself can thus be seen as the "two horns" who have merged, the woman who has become the androgyn, able to procreate of her own accord. She has succeeded in the initiation of

---

*See Rigoglioso, *Cult of Divine Birth*, 20, where I discuss an excerpt from the Nag Hammadi text *The Revelation of Adam*, which reveals that the female who conceives parthenogenetically must first become "androgynous."

the "inner" bridal chamber. Thus at this point in her expanded state journey she is touching the Unicorn because, through her own inner spiritual unification, she is one and the same with this being. The dualities of yin and yang, right and left, flesh and spirit, are resolved into Sovereignty and Wholeness.

The Virgin therefore mirrors the Unicorn, and the Unicorn mirrors her. This is dramatically underscored in a fifth panel, referred to as "sight," where the Sacred Virgin literally shows the Unicorn its own image in a mirror. The mystical being and the lady are one and the same, they are both spiritually complete, and it is time for both of them to bask in this realization. What's more, this happens as the Unicorn sits blissfully in the Sacred Virgin's lap, with her arm encircling its neck. This tells us that this unification has taken place through the power of the Holy Womb of the Great Mother herself.

What is important here is that the mirroring goes beyond the lady and the Unicorn. In holding up the looking glass to this elevated creature, the Sacred Virgin is holding it up to each of us, telling us, "All you need do is grasp the unity within that is already your birthright."

We have now arrived at a sixth panel, where the Sacred Virgin stands alone under a decorative tent. Over a jewelry box her hands grasp a necklace of the kind she has been wearing throughout the journey. Whether she is taking it off or putting it on again with a new attitude is unclear, but what is unmistakable are the words emblazoned over the canopy: "My Sole Desire." Having understood the meaning of the mirror, the significance of this panel, depicting the sense of "intuition," becomes even more clear—and something whose message becomes translatable to all of us. In medieval France the sixth sense was also seen to be the inward sense of the heart, which was meant to tame all the other senses.[26] Thus for the Sacred Virgin of this great mystery cycle, the intuition she has accessed is a wisdom that is imbued with love. In this she has achieved the kind of love that is the very province of Mary, whose name, again, comes from the Egyptian concept of *Meri*, Divine Love, the one who is both Lover and Beloved.

The fact that the Sacred Virgin has achieved an inner unification culminating in love helps us understand the meaning of the words "My Sole Desire." Some have conjectured that they are a plea for, or a message to, an earthly lover. But we can see that the tent is meant only for one. There is no room for a lover, nor is there an invitation to one through a chair, bed, or other symbol. Rather, in this final tableau the Sacred Virgin has accomplished her inner alchemical marriage in the "bridal chamber." She has achieved supreme sovereignty—that is, unification with Divine Mother/Mother Mary. No truer love can there be, and therefore no greater desire can there be. Whether from here the Sacred Virgin wishes to join in sacred union with another is thus her choice, but surely any such union will be far more successful owing to the fact that she has completed this true initiation unto herself.

On the womb level, Mary achieved this inner alchemy, this sacred marriage, so as literally to be able to conceive within herself and give birth. The tapestry series reminds us that such divine unity is the promise for all of us following the Feminine Mystery Path on the inner planes, even if we are not to conceive children in this way. By undergoing a similar process of opening our senses to the inner dimensions of reality, we may re-birth ourselves at a higher octave, and access the Sacred Heart within. Through this process, we also unite the third dimensional world of the physical body (the senses) with the world of spirit, and we understand and embody the divine consciousness inherent in manifest life itself.[27] We thus bring heaven to Earth—and in doing so, we create the "New Earth."

This tapestry mystery story also tells us that such inner unification can have its positive effect in the outer world, as well. In each panel the Sacred Virgin is accompanied not only by the Unicorn on her left but also by the lion on her right. We learn from the ancient lore, that Unicorns and lions were staunch enemies of one another.[28] Yet, remarkably, in these tableaux they sit or stand peaceably on either side of the maiden, sometimes even smiling. Clearly these great works are showing us what Mother Mary demonstrated—that all enmity can be resolved through inner reconciliation and the application of the Sacred, Loving Heart. This is the realm, the work, and the gift of the initiatory path of the *Meri*. This is what will be needed if the earth plane is to move past the last prophecies of Mary before her departure. And the process can be greatly assisted when we call upon the help, powers, mentoring, and mirroring of the Blessed Mother.

Although the Cloisters tapestries, in contrast to the Cluny series, depict the violent intrusion of the unhealed Masculine into this story—the patriarchal impulse to grab and acquire, rather than spiritually merge with, the Unicorn—the promise of humanity's awakening may not be entirely absent. However, it can be discovered only through an intense scrutiny of the final panel, in which the Unicorn lies reborn, yet still imprisoned.

The only other animal that appears here aside from this being is a tiny frog. It is highly camouflaged in the field of flora that explodes throughout the weaving, but it can be found in the lower right-hand side of the panel.* When I visited the collection some fifteen years ago, the museum guide suggested that this may have been the kind of toad whose skin could cause altered-state journeys when licked. This comment struck me like a bolt of lightning. I knew from my research that toads had indeed been used in this way by none other than the wise medicine women of the Middle Ages who came to be persecuted as witches. This tiny frog was thus my own first glimpse of the Female Mystery story behind the Unicorn and its connection to Mother Mary, one that has been fulfilled only in my exploration of the Cluny tapestries all these years later. Even in the grotesque Cloisters story, where "the lion and the lamb" are at odds, the promise of humanity's awakening may well lie hidden there inconspicuously in the Faerie garden of Mary. By opening our consciousness with the help of the chemicals on the little frog's skin, we can experience a great connection with the

---

*See, for example, Freeman, *The Unicorn Tapestries*, 35, for a glimpse of this curious creature.

realms of the Feminine Divine, see the bigger picture, expand our souls, and live in a way that will support the great awakening of humanity as a whole.

It is fascinating that these dramatic stories are illustrated on woven items, no less. As I discuss extensively in *The Mystery Tradition of Miraculous Conception*, and as I mentioned earlier in this book, Mary herself was a temple weaver—and was, in fact, "weaving" at the time she conceived Jesus. I have suggested that this is referencing an inner working and weaving of her own chromosomes in the egg that sparked the Christ.[29] So it is synchronistically fitting that the story of Mary's sacred mysteries of the womb and heart were depicted on great works of warp and weft.

Given that weaving and embroidery were mainly female arts, we can imagine that these tapestries were created largely, if not entirely, by the hands of women. Who the specific designers were has been lost in the sands of time. But clearly the images drawn upon were being pulled from the deep mystical history related to the Unicorn, the powers of the Female Womb, and Virgin Birth. The potency of these meanings may have been discerned by the most esoteric among the nobles and royals.

These images now appear in the public domain, where they continue to serve as conveyances for the mysteries they both conceal and reveal. They beckon us to enter the Garden of the Faeries, the land of the Unicorn, and the realm of Mary, where perhaps we will find these beings shining before us when we at last achieve our greatest desire—the light body immortalization that is our birthright.

CHAPTER 7 INTEGRATION ACTIVITY

The Sidhe and the Sacred Feminine

You're invited to take your Mary Journal and write down your thoughts related to the following:

• Have you had any connection to the Fae or to Unicorns?

- How has considering Mary's Sidhe qualities changed or expanded your perception of her?
- How do you wish and intend to bring more of these qualities into your own life?
- Have you been through your own mystery initiation into the Sacred Feminine?
- What was that like for you?
- If not, how might you like to call upon Mother Mary to commence such a journey?

·················· Online Guided Meditation ··················

Merging with Jesus and Mary in Their Sidhe Valence

In this journey, you will tune into the bright and refreshing Faerie or Sidhe aspect that Jesus and Mary embody. You will be led to understand what that means more deeply and to integrate those beneficial qualities within yourself. See page 150 to register for the free meditations.

The Sacred Order of the Marys and YOU

A Pathway to Inner Divinity

It's now time to get more personal. You've been connecting with Mother Mary throughout this book by learning about suppressed parts of her history, her "secret" life. You've been experiencing her as a healer through the meditations I've offered. Now it's time for you to consider: Are you ready to go further?

By that I mean, are you intrigued about engaging with Mary as a mentor in the art of activating your full spiritual potential? Are you interested in matching her energy to bring yourself into new levels of growth in an exponential way *in this lifetime*? Do you want to become a greater emissary of love, compassion, and wisdom by calling upon Mary as your guide and helper? Are you ready to catapult yourself into the New Earth domain of infinite well-being and creativity that we only have distant memories of on the planet, mostly classified under "legend?"

I believe all this represents the promise Mary offers you. This is about nothing less than the evolution of your soul and our world—and maybe even worlds and dimensions beyond. What I've referred to as the fifth dimension is a domain where the emotional turmoil and suffering has eased, because you have addressed and worked through the agony within you. You've done the healing you need. You've recognized your karma and shadow behaviors in this and other lifetimes, you've acknowledged and brought tenderness to your trauma, and you've honored your grief. Yes, imagine that this is possible.

In chapter 2 I discussed a bit about my own process with this journey, one that can perhaps serve as a reflection or model for your own. Throughout this book, I've offered intriguing insights, as well as tools in the form of healing and empowering guided meditations that will help you release and go deeper. I've mentioned the other resources I offer, which may assist you, as well. These are all wonderful ways to connect with Mother Mary, access her healing powers, and call upon her as a guide for your own awakening and ascension. There are other ways to accomplish this soul growth, as well, some of which you will likely be led to yourself as you put out the call to this great female Master and Goddess.

THE SACRED ORDER OF THE MARYS AS A PATHWAY TO DIVINE LOVE

One way of doing so is to join the Sacred Order of the Marys—and thereby *become* a Mary.

The Sacred Order of the Marys. If you have been tuning into this book and its messages, simply hearing these words is all you need to understand that such an order has always existed. It lives on the inner planes, and it can manifest and thrive on the outer planes.

This is the Order of women of countless generations who are dedicated to experiencing, expressing, and leading with Divine Love. It is the Order of women who hold their Holy Womb Chakras as portals of great power, and who are eager to learn more about this potency and express it in service to humanity and beyond.

The Sacred Order of the Marys. Just thinking on these words can be an inner call, an inner invitation. This is an Order that you may willingly and freely join, without any requirements other than to continue to return to Love as much as possible. It's a self-authorized order—because you already are the Wise Sophia. No one needs to give you a certificate or a degree in this, or permission to pursue it. No money exchanged, no psychic contracts ensnaring you. You may participate in it as much or as little as you like. You may also dissolve your association at any time.

If you like ceremony, however, here is one way in which you may make your membership in this Order "official":

Light a candle.

Envision yourself grounded with
a great taproot into the Earth.

Envision a Temple of Divine Love. Visualize within this Temple a large circle of many, many women who already belong to this Order, holding hands. In the center of the circle is a great grandmother redwood tree that similarly taps deep into the Earth and reaches up to the heavens.

Step into that circle and touch the redwood.

Now utter these words: "I, [your name], now freely join the Sacred Order of the Marys in Spirit. I join this order with the commitment to [state your sacred intention]."

Conclude with the statement: "Mary I am."

Know that the message of your commitment has been carried into Mother Earth and into the Realms to continue to reverberate and support you in this work. You will manifest and express yourself as a priestess of this Order as you are guided.

This is your time. It is now. These coming years. The global shake-ups have already been happening, and we're not likely to see this go into reverse. So how will you use this as an initiation time for yourself? Are you willing to call upon your own Mary self, your Sophia-Christ light so as to usher in the New Earth, the mode of being in which peace is the order of the day and love is the currency? The world in which we speak truth with kindness, no matter what the inner or outer pressures are that we face, regardless of financial fears and our own trauma triggers? The place where happiness emerges from within? The domain in which creativity is exponential?

This is what working with the newly uncloaked Mother Mary can offer. Hers is but one pathway, but it is a very good one. She has been here for a long time, and she is available to help.

EPILOGUE INTEGRATION ACTIVITY

Deepening the Connection

We've come to the end of this exploration with Mother Mary. I invite you to journal about the following:

- Do you wish to deepen your own personal connection with Mary?
- If so, what does this look like?
- What are your intentions for yourself and your hopes for your relationships with others in doing so?
- Is there a bigger ministry within you awaiting manifestation?

.... Online Guided Meditation ....

Activate Your Unity & Harmony Codes with Mother Mary

With Mother Mary as your guide, you will learn how to pluck the strings of your most benevolent and advanced genetic codings that have been gifted to you from our starry allies. Experience enhanced well-being and foster greater communion and love on earth. Take a deep dive into your DNA and discover what it means to work with Mary in this exciting, intimate way. Tune into the power of Mary as the Master Weaver of the Universe. See page 150 to register for the free meditations.

Additional Teachings
from the Author

*Accessing the Meditations, Engaging in
the Seven Sisters Mystery School Community,
and Other Resources*

To be kept abreast of my continuing work on the Blessed Mother and to access online courses and resources I offer about Mother Mary, Mary Magdalene, the Holy Womb Chakra, and topics relevant to what you've read here, please visit my online school, Seven Sisters Mystery School, at **SevenSistersMysterySchool.com**.

Feel free to explore our offerings, sign up for our Sacred Sunday e-News, and even book a reading or spiritual mentoring session with me.

GUIDED MEDITATIONS

To gain free access to the beautiful collection of guided meditations accompanying each chapter of this book, register at **SevenSistersMysterySchool.com/Mary-book-meditations**. Sign in there and bookmark the thank you page you receive so that you can always readily access it. You may also want to go deeper into the meditation process by spending some time writing about your experiences in your Mary Journal.

FACEBOOK COMMUNITY

Now that you've been through this journey, if you've been shy up until now we hope that you'll muster up the courage to share on the Seven Sisters Mystery School Facebook page at **facebook.com/ SevenSistersMysterySchool**. We'd love to hear your thoughts or experiences related to the integration activities, guided meditations, or any other aspects of what's been presented in this book. Your offerings are valued and will contribute to new global understandings of Mother Mary as Goddess, Priestess, Healer, Spiritual Mentor—and mirror to your own awakening soul.

BOOKS BY THE AUTHOR

The Mystery Tradition of Miraculous Conception: Mary and the Lineage of Virgin Births
The Cult of Divine Birth in Ancient Greece
Virgin Mother Goddesses of Antiquity

Notes

Ancient Greek and Roman references are cited by author, title, and section, following the common scholarly format for citing such. These texts can easily be looked up in various print and online sources.

1. WHY MOTHER MARY IS WORTH REDISCOVERING

1. Barnstone and Meyer, Gospel of Philip, in *Gnostic Bible*, 266.
2. Barnstone and Meyer, Gospel of Philip, in *Gnostic Bible*, 270–71.

2. MARY'S REMOTHERING OF ME

1. Rigoglioso, "Awakening to the Goddess."
2. Rigoglioso, *Cult of Divine Birth*, 132.

3. MARY AS A CONSCIOUS PRIESTESS OF DIVINE BIRTH

1. Bamford, *Isis Mary Sophia*, 100.
2. Bamford, *Isis Mary Sophia*, 52–53; 211.

4. THE POWER OF MARY'S HOLY WOMB CHAKRA—AND YOURS

1. Blavatsky, *Secret Doctrine Dialogues*, 319–20.
2. Kaleshwar, *Real Life*, 61.
3. Kaleshwar, *Real Life*, 141–42.
4. Kaleshwar, *Real Life*, 278.
5. Kaleshwar, *Real Life*, 61.
6. Kaleshwar, *Real Life*, 278.

7. Krymow, *Mary's Flowers*, 21.

8. Kaleshwar, *Real Life*, 70.

9. Kaleshwar, *Real Life*, 33.

10. Kaleshwar, *Real Life*, 70.

11. Kaleshwar, *Real Life*, 69, 75.

12. Kaleshwar, *Real Life*, 70.

13. Kaleshwar, *Real Life*, 61.

14. Kaleshwar, *Real Life*, 62.

15. Kaleshwar, *Real Life*, 63.

16. Kaleshwar, *Real Life*, 64.

17. Kaleshwar, *Real Life*, 71.

18. Rigoglioso, *Mystery Tradition*, 105.

19. Kaleshwar, *Real Life*, 41.

20. Kaleshwar, *Real Life*, 63.

21. Ryan and Ripperger, *Golden Legend*, 523.

22. Kaleshwar, *Real Life*, 63.

23. Kaleshwar, *Real Life*, 63–64.

24. Shoemaker, *Life of the Virgin*, 22.

25. Shoemaker, *Life of the Virgin*, 90.

26. Kaleshwar, *Real Life*, 75.

27. Kaleshwar, *Real Life*, 61–63, 75.

28. Shoemaker, *Life of the Virgin*, 103.

29. Shoemaker, *Life of the Virgin*, 96.

30. Shoemaker, *Life of the Virgin*, 101, 104.

31. Kaleshwar, *Real Life*, 103, 105–19, 124.

32. Kaleshwar, *Real Life*, 123–24.

33. Mataji et al., *Holy Womb*, 165.

34. Rigoglioso, *Mystery Tradition*, 23–24.

35. Shoemaker, *Life of the Virgin*, 112–20.

36. Kaleshwar, *Real Life*, 124.

37. Mataji et al., *Holy Womb*, 149.

38. Kaleshwar, *Real Life*, 129–31.

39. Kaleshwar, *Real Life*, 41.

40. Kaleshwar, *Real Life*, 43–45.

41. Kateusz, *Mary and Early Christian Women*, 7.

42. James, Gospel of Bartholomew, 2.2, in *Apocryphal New Testament*, 170.

5. MARY AS HEALER, MENTOR, AND WOMEN'S CHAMPION

1. Kateusz, *Mary and Early Christian Women*, 5–12.

2. Kateusz, *Mary and Early Christian Women*, 19–21.

3. Kateusz, *Mary and Early Christian Women*, 10–11.

4. Kateusz, *Mary and Early Christian Women*, 45.

5. Kateusz, *Mary and Early Christian Women*, 37.

6. Kateusz, *Mary and Early Christian Women*, 9, 26.

7. James, Gospel of Bartholomew, 4.2, in *Apocryphal New Testament*, 173.

8. Kateusz, *Mary and Early Christian Women*, 8.

9. Kateusz, *Mary and Early Christian Women*, 8.

10. Shoemaker, *Life of the Virgin*, 97, 101, 102.

11. Shoemaker, *Life of the Virgin*, 22.

12. Shoemaker, *Life of the Virgin*, 90.

13. Shoemaker, *Life of the Virgin*, 103–21.

14. Kateusz, *Mary and Early Christian Women*, 25.

15. Kateusz, *Mary and Early Christian Women*, 21, 24, 47.

16. Shoemaker, *Life of the Virgin*, 121–26.

17. Shoemaker, *Life of the Virgin*, 128.

18. Kateusz, *Mary and Early Christian Women*, 48.

19. Budge, *History of the Blessed Virgin Mary*, 97.

20. Shoemaker, *Life of the Virgin*, 96.

21. Shoemaker, *Life of the Virgin*, 98.

22. Budge, *History of the Blessed Virgin Mary*, 99.

23. Budge, *History of the Blessed Virgin Mary*, 99.

24. Budge, *History of the Blessed Virgin Mary*, 99.

25. Budge, *History of the Blessed Virgin Mary*, 99.

26. Bible Hub, Gospel of Pseudo-Matthew, chapter 42.

27. Bible Hub, Gospel of Pseudo-Matthew, chapter 42, note 1690.

28. Budge, *History of the Blessed Virgin Mary*, 16.

29. Bible Hub, Gospel of Pseudo-Matthew, chapter 42 and note 1690.

30. Kim, *Fathers of the Church*, 144.

31. Shoemaker, *Life of the Virgin*, 98–99.

32. Shoemaker, *Life of the Virgin*, 99.

33. Shoemaker, *Life of the Virgin*, 98–99.

34. Meyer, *Gospels of Mary,* 109, note 47.

35. Barnstone and Meyer, "Thunder," in *Gnostic Bible*, 226.

36. Rigoglioso, *Miraculous Conception*, 111.
37. Starbird, *Woman with the Alabaster Jar*, 27.
38. Starbird, *Woman with the Alabaster Jar*, 59–62.
39. See Teubal, *Sarah the Priestess*, throughout.
40. Kaleshwar, *Real Life*, 129–31.
41. Bible Hub, Gospel of Pseudo-Matthew, chapter 42.
42. Shoemaker, *Life of the Virgin*, 48.
43. Shoemaker, *Life of the Virgin*, 48.
44. Shoemaker, *Life of the Virgin*, 97.
45. See Shoemaker, *Life of the Virgin*, 97.
46. *Encyclopaedia Britannica Online*, Academic ed., s.v. "Saint James"; see also Shoemaker, *Life of the Virgin*, 125.
47. Shoemaker, *Life of the Virgin*, 98, 120, 125.

6. MARY'S FULL ASCENSION TO DIVINITY

1. Kateusz, *Mary and Early Christian Women*, 26.
2. Wright, "Departure of My Lady," 133. (Wright's translation of *Six Books*.)
3. Shoemaker, *Life of the Virgin*, 128.
4. Shoemaker, *Life of the Virgin*, 132, 152.
5. Wright, "Departure of My Lady," 136–40.
6. Wright, "Departure of My Lady," 138.
7. Wright, "Departure of My Lady," 141.
8. See Huggins, "Legends of Mount Diablo," 129–35.
9. Cowell Historical Society, "Legends of the 'Devil' Mountain."
10. Wright, "Departure of My Lady," 147.
11. Wright, "Departure of My Lady," 148.
12. Kateusz, *Mary and Early Christian Women*, 138–39; and Rigoglioso, *Mystery Tradition*, 102.
13. Kateusz, *Mary and Early Christian Women*, 35.
14. Wright, "Departure of My Lady," 150.
15. Wright, "Departure of My Lady," 152.
16. Wright, "Departure of My Lady," 152.
17. Wright, "Departure of My Lady," 152.
18. Wright, "Departure of My Lady," 157.
19. Wright, "Departure of My Lady," 130.
20. Wright, "Departure of My Lady," 158.
21. Wright, "Departure of My Lady," 158.

22. Wright, "Departure of My Lady," 159.

23. Shoemaker, *Life of the Virgin*, 136.

24. Shoemaker, *Life of the Virgin*, 132 and 141.

7. MARY'S CONNECTION TO THE SUBTLE ANGELICS OF NATURE

1. Krymow, *Mary's Flowers,* 16.

2. Hancock, *Visionary*, 362. I thank Alessanda Gilioli for bringing this to my attention.

3. Spangler, *Conversations with the Sidhe*, 1.

4. Spangler, *Conversations with the Sidhe*, 71–72.

5. Spangler, *Conversations with the Sidhe*, 72.

6. Personal email correspondence from David Spangler, December 30, 2018.

7. White, "Resurrection and the Body of Light," 11.

8. Rigoglioso, *Mystery Tradition*, 79–80.

9. Williams, *Reality, Mythology, and Fantasies*, 79; see also Boehm, *Blessing of Unicorns,* 9.

10. Williams, *Reality, Mythology, and Fantasies*, 81.

11. Boehm, *Blessing of Unicorns*, 10.

12. Williams, *Reality, Mythology, and Fantasies*, 81.

13. Freeman, *Unicorn Tapestries*, 8.

14. Boehm, *Blessing of Unicorns*, 13.

15. Boehm, *Blessing of Unicorns*, 14.

16. Cavallo, *Unicorn Tapestries*, 24, and Wischnewsky, "Unicorn in Stained Glass."

17. *Britannica*, "Unicorn"; see also Williams, *Reality, Mythology, and Fantasies*, 82–83, and Boehm, *Blessing of Unicorns*, 9.

18. Freeman, *Unicorn Tapestries*, 2.

19. Freeman, *Unicorn Tapestries*, 46.

20. Williams, *Reality, Mythology, and Fantasies*, 81.

21. See Rigoglioso, *Cult of Divine Birth*, 6, 72–73, 146; and *Mystery Tradition*, 15–16.

22. Boehm, *Blessing of Unicorns*, 36; see also Cavallo, *Unicorn Tapestries*, 94–99, for high-quality color renderings of these panels.

23. Rigoglioso, *Mystery Tradition*, 85.

24. Rigoglioso, *Mystery Tradition*, 131.

25. Krymow, *Mary's Flowers*, 21–22.

26. Boehm, *Blessing of Unicorns,* 37.

27. I thank artist Tom Schneider for this insight.

28. Brenman and Colasuonno, *Book of the Magical, Mythical Unicorn*, 69.

29. Rigoglioso, *Mystery Tradition*, 101.

Bibliography

Bamford, Christopher, ed. *Isis Mary Sophia: Her Mission and Ours. Selected Lectures and Writings by Rudolph Steiner.* Great Barrington, MA: SteinerBooks, 2003.

Barnstone, Willis, and Marvin Meyer, eds. *The Gnostic Bible.* Boston & London: Shambala, 2003.

Bauckham, Richard. *Jude and the Relatives of Jesus in the Early Church.* London: Bloomsbury, 2015.

Berg, Wendy. *Red Tree, White Tree: Faeries and Humans in Partnership.* Cheltenham, UK: Skylight Press, 2010.

Bible Hub. Gospel of Pseudo-Matthew, chapter 42, Bible Hub website.

———. *Strong's Concordance* 3137, "Maria or Mariam," Bible Hub website.

Bible Probe. *Transitus Mariae*, Bible Probe website.

Blackman, Sushila. *Graceful Exits: How Great Beings Die: Death Stories of Tibetan, Hindu and Zen Masters.* New York: Weatherhill, 1997.

Blavatsky, H. P. *The Secret Doctrine Dialogues.* Los Angeles: The Theosophical Society, 2014.

Boehm, Barbara Drake. "A Blessing of Unicorns: The Paris and Cloisters Tapestries." *Metropolitan Museum of Art Bulletin* 78, no. 1 (Summer 2020).

Bourgeault, Cynthia. *The Meaning of Mary Magdalene: Discovering the Woman at the Heart of Christianity.* Boulder, CO: Shambhala, 2010.

Brenman, Vakasha, and Alfonso Colasuonno. *The Book of the Magical, Mythical Unicorn.* Winchester, UK: O-Books, 2020.

Budge, E.A. Wallis. *The History of the Blessed Virgin Mary and the History of the Likeness of Christ.* London: Luzac & Co, 1899. Archive.org website.

Cavallo, Adolpho Salvatore. *The Unicorn Tapestries at the Metropolitan Museum of Art.* New York: Harry M. Abrams, Inc., 1998.

Cowell Historical Society. "Legends of the 'Devil' Mountain of California." Cowell Historical Society website.

Cromby, R. Ogilvie. *The Gentleman and the Faun*. Findhorn, Scotland: Findhorn Press, 2009.

Cross, Frank Leslie, and Elizabeth A. Livingstone. "James, St., 'the Great.'" *The Oxford Dictionary of the Christian Church*, third edition. Oxford: Oxford University Press, 2009. Available on Oxford Reference website.

Dowman, Keith. "Motivation of the Lay Pilgrim," from *The Sacred Life of Tibet*. London: Thorsons (HarperCollins), 1997. Available on Keith Dowman's website.

Ephesus. "The Virgin Mary's House," Ephesus website.

Freeman, Margaret. *The Unicorn Tapestries*. Monograph of the Metropolitan Museum of New York, 1974.

Froud, Brian. *The Fairies Oracle*. New York: Simon & Schuster, 2000.

Geni. "Jean I, seigneur de La Rochefoucauld." Geni website.

Grant, Robert. *Gnosticism*. New York: Harper and Rowe, 1961.

Gyaltsen, Shardza Tasha. *Heart Drops of Dharmakaya: Dzogchen Practice of the Bon Tradition*, 2nd ed. Ithaca, NY: Snow Lion Publications, 2002.

Hancock, Graham. *Visionary: The Mysterious Origins of Human Consciousness*. Newburyport, MA: New Page Books, 2022.

Heartsong, Claire. *Anna, Grandmother of Jesus*. London: Hay House, 2017.

———. *Anna, the Voice of the Magdalenes*. London: Hay House, 2017.

Holland, Gail. "The Rainbow Body." *IONS Review* 59 (March–May 2002).

Huggins, Dorothy. "The Legends of Mount Diablo." *Western Folklore* 7, no. 2 (April 1948).

James, Montague Rhodes, trans. *The Apocryphal New Testament*. Oxford: Clarendon Press, 1924. Archive.org website.

Jones, Jeannette D. "A Theological Interpretation of 'Viriditas' in Hildegard of Bingen and Gregory the Great." Portfolio of the Department of Musicology and Ethnomusicology at Boston University, vol. 1, December 10th, 2012. Boston University website.

Kaleshwar, Sri. *The Real Life and Teachings of Jesus Christ*. Penukonda, India: Sri Kaleshwar Publications, 2010.

———. Sri Kaleshwar websites: Sri Kaleshwar Ashram and Kaleshwar.org.

Kateusz, Ally. *Mary and Early Christian Women: Hidden Leadership*. New York: Palgrave Macmillan, 2019.

Kim, Young Richard. *The Fathers of the Church: A New Translation*. Vol. 128. Washington, D.C.: Catholic University of America Press, 2014.

King, Karen. *The Gospel of Mary of Magdala: Jesus and the First Woman Apostle.* Santa Rosa, CA: Polebridge Press, 2003.

Krymow, Vincenzina. *Mary's Flowers: Gardens, Legends, and Meditations.* Phoenix, AZ: Faith & Flowers, 1999.

Lindahl, Cort. "The Rochefoucauld family, the Holy Grail and Oak Island." December 1, 2022. Historical Mysteries in Geography and Architecture website.

Mataji (Monika Penukonda), Sri Sai Kaleshwara Swami, and Sri Kaleshwar. *The Holy Womb: The Secrets of the Divine Mother's Creation.* 2nd ed. Laytonville, CA: Divine Mother Center, October 2020.

McAfee, John. *Beyond the Siddhis: Supernatural Powers and the Sutras of Patanjali.* Woodland Park, CO: Woodland Publications, 2001.

Meyer, Marvin. *The Gospels of Mary.* San Francisco: HarperSanFrancisco, 2004.

Monica of Penukonda. "The Divine Mission" and other articles. Monika of Penukonda website.

Office de Tourisme de La Rochefoucauld, Porte du Perigord. "La Rochefoucauld over 1000 years of history." Office de Tourisme de La Rochefoucauld, Porte du Perigord website.

Poitras, Den. *Parthenogenesis: Women's Long-Lost Ability to Self-Conceive.* Self-published, 2018.

Prakash, S. *Prashna Kundali and Saptarishis in Manvantara and Yugas: Plan of Brahma in Creation of Universe.* Amazon Digital Services, 2022.

Reenu, Namita. "Why St. Hildegard's Spirituality of 'Viriditas' Is Extraordinary." Global Sisters Report website.

Rigoglioso, Marguerite. "Awakening to the Goddess." *New Age Journal* May/June 1997: 60–69, 138–50.

———. *Bearing the Holy Ones: A Study of the Cult of Divine Birth in Ancient Greece.* Ph.D. diss., California Institute of Integral Studies, San Francisco, 2007. Dissertation Abstracts International, publ. nr. ATT 3286688, DAI-A 68/10 (April 2008).

———. *The Cult of Divine Birth in Ancient Greece.* New York: Palgrave Macmillan, 2009.

———. *The Mystery Tradition of Miraculous Conception: Mary and the Lineage of Virgin Births.* Rochester, VT: Bear & Company, 2021.

———. *Virgin Mother Goddesses of Antiquity.* New York: Palgrave Macmillan, 2010.

Ryan, Granger, and Helmut Ripperger, eds. *The Golden Legend of Jacobus de Voragine.* New York: Arno Press. 1969.

Shoemaker, Stephen J., trans. *The Life of the Virgin: Maximus the Confessor.* New Haven: Yale University Press, 2012.

Spangler, David. *Conversations with the Sidhe.* Camano Island, WA: Lorian Press, 2014.

Spretnak, Charlene. *Missing Mary: The Queen of Heaven and Her Re-Emergence in the Modern Church.* New York: Palgrave Macmillan, 2004.

————. *The Politics of Women's Spirituality: Essays by Founding Mothers of the Movement.* New York: Knopf Doubleday Publishing Group, 1982.

Starbird, Margaret. *The Woman with the Alabaster Jar: Mary Magdalene and the Holy Grail.* Rochester, VT: Bear & Company, 1993.

Teubal, Savina J. *Sarah the Priestess: The First Matriarch of Genesis.* Athens, OH: Swallow Press, 1984.

Walton O'Brien, Maureen. *The Good Darkness: Wisdom of the Womb Blood.* Self-published, 2022.

Wayne, Luke. "The Quran, the Crucifixion, and the Gnostics." Christian Apologetics and Research Ministry (CARM) website, July 11, 2016.

White, John. "Resurrection and the Body of Light." *Quest Magazine* 97, no. I (Fall 2009): 11–15. The Theosophical Society website.

Wilkins, William Joseph (1882) 1913. *Hindu Mythology, Vedic and Puranic.* 3rd ed. Calcutta: London Missionary Society. Archive.org website.

Williams, W.B.J. *The Reality, Mythology, and Fantasies of Unicorns.* Dragonwell Publishing, 2001.

Wischnewsky, Jenny. "The Unicorn in Stained Glass." *Vidimus* 75 (December 2013).

Wright, William, trans. "The Departure of My Lady from This World." *Journal of the Sacred Literature and Biblical Record* VII (1865): 129–60. Available on The Wayback Machine, University of Oregon website. (Note: this is Wright's translation of *Six Books.*)

Yogananda, Paramahansa. *Autobiography of a Yogi.* Los Angeles: Self-Realization Fellowship, 1997.

Yogoda Satsanga Society of India. "Final Years and Mahasamhadi." Yogoda Satsanga Society of India website.

Index